KT-476-872

Breads & Baking

Quick and Easy, Proven Recipes

FLAME TREE
PUBLISHING

Contents

Contents

Biscuits, Cookies, Brownies & Traybakes

Contents

Everyday Cakes & Buns   262

Essential Ingredients

The quantities may differ, but basic baking ingredients do not vary greatly. Let us take a closer look at the baking ingredients which are essential.

Fat

Butter and firm block margarine are the fats most commonly used in baking. Others can also be used such as white vegetable fat, lard and oil. Low-fat spreads are not recommended as they break down when cooked at a high temperature and are not recommended for baking. Often it is a matter of personal preference which fat you choose when baking but there are a few guidelines that are important to remember.

Unsalted butter is the fat most commonly used in cake making, especially in rich fruit cakes and the heavier sponge cakes such as Madeira or chocolate torte. Unsalted butter gives a distinctive flavour to the cake. Some people favour margarine which imparts little or no flavour to the cake. As a rule, firm margarine and butter should not be used straight from the refrigerator but allowed to come to room temperature before using. Also, it should be beaten by itself first before creaming or rubbing in. Soft margarine is best suited to one-stage recipes. If oil is used care should be taken – it is a good idea to follow a specific recipe as the proportions of oil to flour and eggs are different.

Fat is an integral ingredient when making pastry, again there are a few specific guidelines to bear in mind.

For shortcrust pastry the best results are achieved by using equal amounts of lard or white vegetable fat with butter or block margarine. The amount of fat used is always half the amount of flour. Other pastries use differing amounts of ingredients. Pâté sucrée (a sweet flan pastry) uses all butter with eggs and a little sugar, while flaky or puff pastry uses a larger proportion of fat to flour and relies on the folding and rolling during making to ensure that the pastry rises and flakes well. When using a recipe, refer to the instructions to obtain the best result.

Flour

We can buy a wide range of flour all designed for specific jobs. Strong flour which is rich in gluten, whether it is white or brown (this includes granary and stoneground) is best kept for bread and Yorkshire pudding. It is also recommended for steamed suet puddings as well as puff pastry. '00' flour is designed for pasta making and there is no substitute for this

flour. Ordinary flour or weak flour is best for cakes, biscuits and sauces which absorb the fat easily and give a soft light texture. This flour comes in plain white or self-raising, as well as wholemeal. Self-raising flour, which has the raising agent already incorporated is best kept for sponge cakes where it is important that an even rise is achieved. Plain flour can be used for all types of baking and sauces. If using plain flour for scones or cakes and puddings, unless other-wise stated in the recipe, use 1 teaspoon of baking powder to 225 g/8 oz of plain flour. With sponge cakes and light fruit cakes, it is best to use self-raising flour as the raising agent has already been added to the flour. This way there is no danger of using too much which can result in a sunken cake with a sour taste. There are other raising agents that are also used. Some cakes use bicarbonate of soda with or without cream of tartar, blended with warm or sour milk. Whisked eggs also act as a raising agent as the air trapped in the egg ensures that the mixture rises. Generally no other raising agent is required.

Flour also comes ready sifted. There is even a special sponge flour designed especially for whisked sponges. Also, it is possible to buy flours that cater for coeliacs which contain no gluten. Buckwheat, soya and chick pea flours are also available.

Eggs

When a recipe states 1 egg, it is generally accepted this refers to a medium egg. Over the past few years the grading of eggs has changed. For years, eggs were sold as small, standard and large, then this method changed and they were graded in numbers with 1 being the largest. The general feeling by the public was that this system was misleading, so now we buy our eggs as small, medium and large. Due to the slight risk of salmonella, all eggs are now sold date stamped to ensure that the eggs are used in their prime. This applies even to farm eggs which are no longer allowed to be sold straight from the farm. Look for the lion quality stamp (on 75% of all eggs sold) which guarantees that the eggs come from hens vaccinated against salmonella, have been laid in the UK and are produced to the highest food safety and standards. All of these eggs carry a best before date.

There are many types of eggs sold and it really is a question of personal preference which ones are chosen. All offer the same nutritional benefits. The majority of eggs sold in this country are caged eggs. These are the cheapest eggs and the hens have been fed on a manufactured mixed diet.

Barn eggs are from hens kept in barns who are free to roam within the barn. However, their diet is similar to caged hens and the barns may be overcrowded.

It is commonly thought that free-range eggs are from hens that lead a much more natural life and are fed natural foods.

This, however, is not always the case and in some instances they may still live in a crowded environment.

Four-grain eggs are from hens that have been fed on grain and no preventative medicines have been included in their diet.

Organic eggs are from hens that live in a flock, whose beaks are not clipped and who are completely free to roam. Obviously, these eggs are much more expensive than the others.

Store eggs in the refrigerator with the round end uppermost (as packed in the egg boxes). Allow to come to room temperature before using. Do remember, raw or semi-cooked eggs should not be given to babies, toddlers, pregnant women, the elderly and those suffering from a reccurring illness.

Sugar

Sugar not only offers taste to baking but also adds texture and volume to the mixture. It is generally accepted that caster sugar is best for sponge cakes, puddings and meringues. Its fine granules disperse evenly when creaming or whisking. Granulated sugar is used for more general cooking, such as stewing fruit, whereas demerara sugar with its toffee taste and crunchy texture is good for sticky puddings and cakes such as flapjacks. For rich fruit cakes, Christmas puddings and cakes, use the muscovado sugars which give a rich intense molasses or treacle flavour. Icing sugar is used primarily for icings and can be used in meringues and in fruit sauces when the sugar needs to dissolve

quickly. For a different flavour try flavouring your own sugar. Place a vanilla pod in a screw top jar, fill with caster sugar, screw down the lid and leave for 2–3 weeks before using. Top up after use or use thinly pared lemon or orange rind in the same manner.

If trying to reduce sugar intake then use the unrefined varieties, such as golden granulated, golden caster, unrefined demerara and the muscovado sugars. All of these are a little sweeter than their refined counterparts, so less is required. Alternatively, clear honey or fructose (fruit sugar) can reduce sugar intake as they have similar calories to sugar, but are twice as sweet. Also, they have a slow release so their effect lasts longer. Dried fruits can also be included in the diet to top up sugar intake.

Yeast

There is something very comforting about the aroma of freshly baked bread and the taste is far different and superior to commercially made bread. Bread making is regarded by some as being a time consuming process but with the advent of fast-acting yeast this no longer applies. There are three types of yeast available, fresh yeast, which can now be bought in the Instore bakery department of many supermarkets (fresh yeast freezes well), dried yeast which is available in tins and quick-acting yeast which comes in packets.

Fresh yeast should be bought in small quantities; it has a putty-like colour and texture with a slight wine smell. It should be creamed with a little sugar and some warm liquid before being added to the flour.

Dried yeast, can be stored for up to six months and comes in small hard granules. It should be sprinkled on to warm liquid with a little sugar then left to stand, normally between 15–20 minutes, until the mixture froths. When replacing the fresh yeast with dried yeast, use 1 tablespoon of dried yeast for 25 g/1 oz of fresh yeast.

Quick acting yeast cuts down the time of bread making and eliminates the need for proving the bread twice. Also, the yeast can be added straight to the flour without it needing to be activated. When replacing quick-acting yeast for dried yeast, you will need double the amount.

When using yeast the most important thing to remember is that yeast is a living plant and needs food, water and warmth to work.

Equipment

Nowadays, you can get lost in the cookware sections of some of the larger stores – they really are a cook's paradise with gadgets, cooking tools and state-of-the-art electronic blenders, mixers and liquidisers. A few, well-picked, high-quality utensils and pieces of equipment will be frequently used and will therefore be a much wiser buy than cheaper gadgets.

Cooking equipment not only assists in the kitchen, but can make all the difference between success and failure. Take the humble cake tin, although a very basic piece of cooking equipment, it plays an essential role in baking. Using the incorrect size, for example, a tin that is too large will spread the mixture too thinly and the result will be a flat, limp-looking cake. On the other hand, cramming the mixture into a tin which is too small will result in the mixture rising up and out of the tin.

Baking Equipment

To ensure successful baking it is worth investing in a selection of high quality tins, which if looked after properly should last for many years. Follow the manufacturers' instructions when first using and ensure that the tins are thoroughly washed and dried after use and before putting away.

Perhaps the most useful of tins for baking are sandwich cake tins, ideal for classics such as Victoria sponge, genoese and coffee and walnut cake. You will need two tins and they are normally 18 cm/7 inches or 20.5 cm/8 inches in diameter and are about 5–7.5cm/2–3 inches deep and are often non stick.

With deep cake tins, it is personal choice whether you buy round or square tins and they vary in size from 12.5–35.5 cm /5–14 inches with a depth of between 12.5–15 cm/5–6 inches. A deep cake tin, for everyday fruit or Madeira cake is a must, a useful size is 20.5 cm/8 inches.

Loaf tins are used for bread, fruit or tea bread and terrines and normally come in two sizes, 450 g/1 lb and 900 g/2 lb.

Good baking sheets are a must for all cooks. Dishes that are too hot to handle such as apple pies should be placed directly on to the baking tray. Meringues, biscuits and cookies are cooked on the tray. Do not confuse with Swiss roll tins which have sides all around, whereas a sheet only has one raised side.

Square or oblong shallow baking tins are also very useful for making tray bakes, fudge brownies, flapjacks and shortbread.

Then there are patty tins; ideal for making small buns, jam tarts or mince pies; individual Yorkshire pudding tins and muffin tins or flan tins. They are available in a variety of sizes.

There are plenty of other tins to choose from, ranging from themed tins, such as a Christmas trees, numbers from 1–9 as well as tins shaped as petals, ring mould tins, (tins with a hole in the centre) to spring form tins where the sides release after cooking allowing the finished cake to be removed easily.

Three to four different sizes of mixing bowls are also very useful.

Another piece of equipment which is worth having is a wire cooling rack. It is essential when baking to allow biscuits and cakes to cool after being removed from their tins.

A selection of different sized roasting tins are also a worthwhile investment as they can double up as a bain marie, or for cooking larger quantities of cakes such as gingerbread. A few different tins and dishes are required if baking crumbles, soufflés and pies. Ramekin dishes and small pudding basins can be used for a variety of different recipes as can small tartlet tins and dariole moulds.

When purchasing your implements for baking, perhaps the rolling pin is one of the most important. Ideally it should be long and thin, heavy enough to roll the pastry out easily but not too heavy that it is uncomfortable to use. Pastry needs to be rolled out on a flat surface and although a lightly floured flat surface will do, a marble slab will ensure that the pastry is kept cool and ensures that the fats do not melt while being rolled. This helps to keep the pastry light, crisp and flaky rather than heavy and stodgy which happens if the fat melts before being baked.

Other useful basic pastry implements are tools such as a pastry brush (which can be used to wet pastry or brush on a glaze), a pastry wheel for cutting and a sieve to remove impurities and also to sift air into the flour, encouraging the pastry or mixture to be lighter in texture.

Basic mixing cutlery is also essential such as a wooden spoon (for mixing and creaming), a spatula (for transferring the mixture from the mixing bowl to the baking tins and spreading the mixture once it is in the tins) and a palette knife (to ease cakes and breads out of their tins before placing them on the wire racks to cool). Measuring spoons are essential for accurate measuring of both dry and wet ingredients.

Electrical Equipment

Nowadays help from time-saving gadgets and electrical equipment make baking far easier and quicker. Equipment can be used for creaming, mixing, beating, whisking and kneading, grating and chopping. There is a wide choice of machines available from the most basic to the very sophisticated.

Food Processors

First decide what you need your processor to do when choosing a machine. If you are a novice to baking, it may be a waste to start with a machine which offers a wide range of implements and functions. This can be off putting and result in not using the machine to its ultimate.

In general, while styling and product design play a role in the price, the more you pay, the larger the machine will be with a bigger bowl capacity and many more gadgets attached. Nowadays, you can chop, shred, slice, chip, blend, purée, knead, whisk and cream anything. However, just what basic features should you ensure your machine has before buying it?

When buying a food processor look for measurements on the side of the processor bowl and machines with a removable feed tube which allows food or liquid to be added while the motor is still running. Look out for machines that have the facility to increase the capacity of the bowl (ideal when making soup) and have a pulse button for controlled chopping.

For many, storage is an issue so reversible discs and flex storage, or on more advanced models, a blade storage compartment or box, can be advantageous.

It is also worth thinking about machines which offer optional extras which can be bought as your cooking requirements change. Mini-chopping bowls are available for those wanting to chop small quantities of food. If time is an issue, dishwasher-friendly attachments may be vital. Citrus presses, liquidisers and whisks may all be useful attachments for the individual cook.

Blenders

Blenders often come as attachments to food processors and are generally used for liquidising and puréeing foods. There are two main types of blender. The first is known as a goblet blender. The blades of this blender are at the bottom of the goblet with measurements up the sides. The second blender is portable. It is hand-held and should be placed in a bowl to blend.

Food Mixers

These are ideally suited to mixing cakes and kneading dough, either as a table-top mixer or a hand-held mixer. Both are extremely useful and based on the same principle of mixing or whisking in an open bowl to allow more air to get to the mixture and therefore give a lighter texture.

The table-top mixers are freestanding and are capable of dealing with fairly large quantities of mixture. They are robust machines, capable of easily dealing with kneading dough and heavy cake mixing as well as whipping cream, whisking egg whites or making one-stage cakes. These mixers also offer a wide range of attachments ranging from liquidisers, mincers, juicers, can openers and many more and varied attachments.

Hand-held mixers are smaller than freestanding mixers and often come with their own bowl and stand from which they can be lifted off and used as hand-held devices. They have a motorised head with detachable twin whisks. These mixers are particularly versatile as they do not need a specific bowl in which to whisk. Any suitable mixing bowl can be used.

Basic Baking Techniques

There is no mystery to successful baking, it really is easy providing you follow a few simple rules and guidelines. First, read the recipe right through before commencing. There is nothing more annoying than getting to the middle of a recipe and discovering that you are minus one or two of the ingredients. Until you are confident, follow a recipe, do not try a short cut otherwise you may find that you have left out a vital step which means that the recipe really cannot work. Most of all, have patience, baking is easy – if you can read, you can bake.

Pastry Making

Pastry needs to be kept as cool as possible through-out. Cool hands help, but are not essential. Use cold or iced water, but not too much as pastry does not need to be wet. Make sure that your fat is not runny or melted but firm (this is why block fat is the best). Avoid using too much flour when rolling out as this alters the proportions and also avoid handling the dough too much. Roll in one direction as this helps to ensure that

Hints for successful baking

Ensure that the ingredients are accurately measured. A cake that has too much flour or insufficient egg will be dry and crumbly. Take care when measuring the raising agent if used, as too much will mean that the cake will rise too quickly and then sink. Insufficient raising agent means the cake will not rise in the first place.

Ensure that the oven is preheated to the correct temperature, it can take 10 minutes to reach 180°C/350°F/Gas Mark 4. You may find that an oven thermometer is a good investment. Cakes are best if cooked in the centre of the preheated oven. Try to avoid opening the oven door at the start of cooking as a draft can make the cake sink. If using a fan oven refer to the manufacturers' instructions.

Check that the cake is thoroughly cooked by removing from the oven and inserting a clean skewer. Leave for 30 seconds and remove. If clean then the cake is cooked, if there is a little mixture return to the oven for a few minutes.

Other problems while cake making are insufficient creaming of the fat and sugar or a curdled creamed mixture (which will result in a fairly solid cake). Flour that has not been folded in carefully enough or has not been mixed with enough raising agent may also result in a fairly heavy consistency. Ensure that the correct size of tin is used as you may end up either with a flat, hard cake or one which has spilled over the edge of the tin. Be aware – especially when cooking with fruit – that if the consistency is too soft, the cake will not be able to support the fruit.

Finally, when you take your cake out of the oven, unless the recipe states that it should be left in the tin until cold, leave for a few minutes, then loosen the edges and turn out on to a wire rack to cool. Cakes which are left in the tin for too long, tend to sink or slightly overcook. When storing, make sure the cake is completely cold before placing it into an airtight tin or plastic container.

the pastry does not shrink. Allow the pastry to rest, preferably in the refrigerator after rolling. If you follow these guidelines but your pastry is still not as good as you would like it to be, then make it in a food processor instead.

Lining a Flan Case

It is important to choose the right tin to bake with. You will often find that a loose-bottomed metal flan case is the best option as it conducts heat more efficiently and evenly than a ceramic dish. It also has the advantage of a removable base which makes transferring the final flan easy; it simply lifts out keeping the pastry intact.

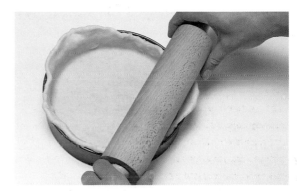

Roll the pastry out on a lightly floured surface ensuring that it is a few inches larger than the flan case. Wrap the pastry round the rolling pin, lift and place in the tin. Carefully ease the pastry into the base and sides of the tin, ensuring that there are no tears in the pastry. Allow to rest for a few minutes then trim the edge either with a sharp knife or by rolling a rolling pin across the top of the flan tin.

Baking Blind

The term baking blind means that the pastry case needs to be cooked without the filling, resulting in a crisp pastry shell that is either partially or fully cooked depending on whether the filling needs any cooking. Pastry shells can be prepared ahead of time as they last for several days if stored correctly in an airtight container or longer if frozen.

To bake blind, line a pastry case with the prepared pastry and allow to rest in the refrigerator for 30 minutes. This will help

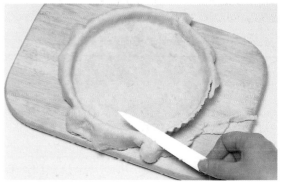

to minimize shrinkage while it is being cooked. Remove from the refrigerator and lightly prick the base all over with a fork (do not do this if the filling is runny). Brush with a little beaten egg if desired or simply line the case with a large square of greaseproof paper, big enough to cover both the base and sides of the pastry case. Fill with either ceramic baking beans or dried beans. Place on a baking sheet and bake in a preheated oven, generally at 200°C/400°F/Gas Mark 6, remembering that ovens can take at least 15 minutes to reach this heat. Cook for 10–12 minutes, then remove from the oven, discard the paper and beans. Return to the oven and continue to cook for a further 5–10 minutes depending on whether the filling needs cooking. Normally, unless otherwise stated, individual pastry tartlet cases also benefit from baking blind.

Covering a Pie Dish

To cover a pie, roll out the pastry until it is about two inches larger than the circumference of the dish. Cut a 2.5 cm/ 1 inch strip from around the outside of the pastry and then moisten the edge of the pie dish you are using. Place the strip on the edge of the dish and brush with water or beaten egg. Generously fill the pie dish until the surface is slightly rounded. Using the rolling pin, lift the remaining pastry and cover the pie dish. Press together, then seal. Using a sharp knife, trim off any excess pastry from around the edges. Try to avoid brushing the edges of the pastry especially puff pastry as this prevents the pastry rising evenly. Before placing in the oven make a small hole in the centre of the pie to allow the steam to escape.

The edges of the pie can be forked by pressing the back of a fork around the edge of the pie or instead crimp by pinching the edge crust holding the thumb and index finger of your right hand against the edge while gently pushing with the index finger of your left hand. Other ways of finishing the pie are to knock up (achieved by gently pressing your index finger down

on to the rim and, at the same time, tapping a knife horizontally along the edge giving it a flaky appearance), or fluting the edges by pressing your thumb down on the edge of the pastry while gently drawing back an all-purpose knife about 1 cm/½ inch and repeating around the rim. Experiment by putting leaves and berries made out of leftover pastry to finish off the pie, then brush the top of the pie with beaten egg.

Lining Cake Tins

If a recipe states that the tin needs lining do not be tempted
to ignore this. Rich fruit cakes and other cakes that take a
long time to cook benefit from the tin being lined so that the
edges and base do not burn or dry out. Greaseproof or baking
parchment paper is ideal for this. It is a good idea to have
the paper at least double thickness, or preferably 3–4
thicknesses. Sponge cakes and other cakes that are cooked
in 30 minutes or less are also better if the bases are lined as
it is far easier to remove them from the tin.

The best way to line a round or square tin is to lightly draw
around the base and then cut just inside the markings making
it easy to sit in the tin. Next, lightly oil the paper so it easily
peels away from the cake. If the sides of the tin also need to
be lined, then cut a strip of paper long enough for the tin. This
can be measured by wrapping a piece of string around the rim
of the tin. Once again, lightly oil the paper, push against the
tin and oil once more as this will hold the paper to the sides
of the tin. Steamed puddings usually need only a disc of
greaseproof paper at the bottom of the dish as the sides
come away easily.

Savoury
Baked Dishes

Fish Puff Tart

SERVES 4

350 g/12 oz prepared puff
pastry, thawed if frozen
150 g/5 oz smoked haddock
150 g/5 oz cod

1 tbsp pesto sauce
2 tomatoes, sliced
125 g/4 oz goats' cheese,
   sliced

1 medium egg, beaten
freshly chopped parsley,
   to garnish

Preheat the oven to 220°C/425°F/Gas Mark 7. On a lightly floured surface roll out the pastry into a 20.5 x 25.5 cm/8 x 10 inch rectangle.

Draw a 18 x 23 cm/7 x 9 inch rectangle in the centre of the pastry, to form a 2.5 cm/1 inch border. (Be careful not to cut through the pastry.) Lightly cut criss-cross patterns in the border of the pastry with a knife.

Place the fish on a chopping board and with a sharp knife skin the cod and smoked haddock. Cut into thin slices.

Spread the pesto evenly over the bottom of the pastry case with the back of a spoon.

Arrange the fish, tomatoes and cheese in the pastry case and brush the pastry with the beaten egg.

Bake the tart in the preheated oven for 20–25 minutes, until the pastry is well risen, puffed and golden brown. Garnish with the chopped parsley and serve immediately.

Try This: FOR AN ALTERNATIVE: 30   FOR A SWEET TREAT: 152

Russian Fish Pie

SERVES 4–6

450 g/1 lb orange roughly or haddock fillet
150 ml/¼ pint dry white wine
salt and freshly ground black pepper
75 g/3 oz butter or margarine
1 large onion, peeled and finely chopped

75 g/3 oz long-grain rice
1 tbsp freshly chopped dill
125 g/4 oz baby button mushrooms, quartered
125 g/4 oz peeled prawns, thawed if frozen
3 medium eggs, hard-boiled and chopped

550 g/1¼ lb ready-prepared puff pastry, thawed if frozen
1 small egg, beaten with a pinch of salt
assorted bitter salad leaves, to serve

Preheat the oven to 200°C/400°F/Gas Mark 6, 15 minutes before cooking. Place the fish in a shallow frying pan with the wine, 150 ml/¼ pint water and salt and pepper. Simmer for 8–10 minutes. Strain the fish, reserving the liquid, and when cool enough to handle, flake into a bowl.

Melt the butter or margarine in a saucepan and cook the onions for 2–3 minutes, then add the rice, reserved fish liquid and dill. Season lightly. Cover and simmer for 10 minutes, then stir in the mushrooms and cook for a further 10 minutes, or until all the liquid is absorbed. Mix the rice with the cooked fish, prawns and eggs. Leave to cool.

Roll half the pastry out on a lightly floured surface into a 23 x 30.5 cm/9 x 12 inch rectangle. Place on a dampened baking sheet and arrange the fish mixture on top, leaving a 1 cm/½ inch border. Brush the border with a little water.

Roll out the remaining pastry to a rectangle and use to cover the fish. Brush the edges lightly with a little of the beaten egg and press to seal. Roll out the pastry trimmings and use to decorate the top. Chill in the refrigerator for 30 minutes. Brush with the beaten egg and bake for 30 minutes, or until golden. Serve immediately with salad leaves.

Try This: FOR AN ALTERNATIVE: 40   FOR A SWEET TREAT: 344

Luxury Fish Pasties

SERVES 6

2 quantities of quick flaky
    pastry (*see* page 92),
    chilled
125 g/4 oz butter
125 g/4oz plain flour
300 ml/½ pint milk
225 g/8 oz salmon fillet,

skinned and cut into
    chunks
1 tbsp freshly chopped
    parsley
1 tbsp freshly chopped dill
grated rind and juice of 1 lime
225 g/8 oz peeled prawns

salt and freshly ground
    black pepper
1 small egg, beaten
1 tsp sea salt
fresh green salad leaves,
    to serve

Preheat the oven to 200°C/400°F/Gas Mark 6. Place the butter in a saucepan and slowly heat until melted. Add the flour and cook, stirring for 1 minute. Remove from the heat and gradually add the milk a little at a time, stirring between each addition.

Return to the heat and simmer, stirring continuously until thickened. Remove from the heat and add the salmon, parsley, dill, lime rind, lime juice, prawns and seasoning.

Roll out the pastry on a lightly floured surface and cut out 6 x 12.5 cm/5 inch circles and 6 x 15 cm/6 inch circles.

Brush the edges of the smallest circle with the beaten egg and place two tablespoons of filling in the centre of each one.

Place the larger circle over the filling and press the edges together to seal. Pinch the edge of the pastry between the forefinger and thumb to ensure a firm seal and decorative edge.

Cut a slit in each parcel, brush with the beaten egg and sprinkle with sea salt. Transfer to a baking sheet and cook in the preheated oven for 20 minutes, or until golden brown. Serve immediately with some fresh green salad leaves.

Try This: FOR AN ALTERNATIVE: 36   FOR A SWEET TREAT: 232

Smoked Mackerel Vol–au–Vents

SERVES 1–2

350 g/12 oz prepared
  puff pastry
1 small egg, beaten
2 tsp sesame seeds
225 g/8 oz peppered smoked

mackerel, skinned
  and chopped
5 cm/2 inch piece cucumber
4 tbsp soft cream cheese
2 tbsp cranberry sauce

1 tbsp freshly chopped dill
1 tbsp finely grated lemon
  rind
dill sprigs, to garnish
mixed salad leaves, to serve

Preheat the oven to 230°C/450°F/Gas Mark 8. Roll the pastry out on a lightly floured surface and using a 9 cm/3½ inch fluted cutter cut out 12 rounds.

Using a 1 cm/½ inch cutter mark a lid in the centre of each round. Place on a damp baking sheet and brush the rounds with a little beaten egg.

Sprinkle the pastry with the sesame seeds and bake in the preheated oven for 10–12 minutes, or until golden brown and well risen.

Transfer the vol-au-vents to a chopping board and when cool enough to touch carefully remove the lids with a small sharp knife. Scoop out any uncooked pastry from the inside of each vol-au-vent, then return to the oven for 5–8 minutes to dry out. Remove and allow to cool.

Flake the mackerel into small pieces and reserve. Peel the cucumber if desired, cut into very small dice and add to the mackerel.

Beat the soft cream cheese with the cranberry sauce, dill and lemon rind. Stir in the mackerel and cucumber and use to fill the vol-au-vents. Place the lids on top and garnish dill sprigs.

Try This: FOR AN ALTERNATIVE: 24   FOR A SWEET TREAT: 188

Smoked Haddock Tart

SERVES 6

Shortcrust pastry:
150 g/5 oz plain flour
pinch of salt
25 g/1 oz lard or white
  vegetable fat, cut into
  small cubes
40 g/1½ oz butter or hard
  margarine, cut into
  small cubes

For the filling:
225 g/8 oz smoked haddock,
  skinned and cubed
2 large eggs, beaten
300 ml/½ pint double cream
1 tsp Dijon mustard
freshly ground black pepper
125 g/4 oz Gruyère
  cheese, grated

1 tbsp freshly snipped chives

To serve:
lemon wedges
tomato wedges
fresh green salad leaves

Preheat the oven to 190°C/375°F/Gas Mark 5. Sift the flour and salt into a large bowl. Add the fats and mix lightly. Using the fingertips rub into the the the mixture until it resembles breadcrumbs.

Sprinkle 1 tablespoon of cold water into the mixture and with a knife, start bringing the dough together. (It may be best to use the hands for the final stage.) If the dough does not form a ball quickly, add a little more water. Put the pastry in a polythene bag and chill for at least 30 minutes.

On a lightly floured surface, roll out the pastry and use to line a 18 cm/7 inch lightly oiled quiche or flan tin. Prick the base all over with a fork and bake blind in the preheated oven for 15 minutes. Carefully remove the pastry from the oven, brush with a little of the beaten egg. Return to the oven for a further 5 minutes, then place the fish in the pastry case.

For the filling, beat together the eggs and cream. Add the mustard, black pepper and cheese and pour over the fish.

Sprinkle with the chives and bake for 35–40 minutes or until the filling is golden brown and set in the centre. Serve hot or cold with the lemon and tomato wedges and salad leaves.

Try This: FOR AN ALTERNATIVE: 78   FOR A SWEET TREAT: 144

Salmon & Filo Parcels

SERVES 4

1 tbsp sunflower oil
1 bunch of spring onions,
   trimmed and finely
   chopped
1 tsp paprika
175 g/6 oz long-grain

white rice
300 ml/½ pint fish stock
salt and freshly ground
   black pepper
450 g/1 lb salmon fillet, cubed
1 tbsp freshly chopped parsley

grated rind and juice of
   1 lemon
150 g/5 oz rocket
150 g/5 oz spinach
12 sheets filo pastry
50 g/2 oz butter, melted

Preheat the oven to 200°C/400°F/Gas Mark 6. Heat the oil in a small frying pan and gently cook the spring onions for 2 minutes. Stir in the paprika and continue to cook for 1 minute, then remove from the heat and reserve.

Put the rice in a sieve and rinse under cold running water until the water runs clear; drain. Put the rice and stock in a saucepan, bring to the boil, then cover and simmer for 10 minutes, or until the liquid is absorbed and the rice is tender. Add the spring onion mixture and fork through. Season to taste with salt and pepper, then leave to cool.

In a non-metallic bowl, mix together the salmon, parsley, lemon rind and juice and salt and pepper. Reserve. Blanch the rocket and spinach for 30 seconds in a large saucepan of boiling water, or until just wilted. Drain well in a colander and refresh in plenty of cold water, then squeeze out as much moisture as possible.

Brush 3 sheets of filo pastry with melted butter and lay them on top of one another. Take a quarter of the rice mixture and arrange it in an oblong in the centre of the pastry. On top of this place a quarter of the salmon followed by a quarter of the rocket and spinach. Draw up the pastry around the filling and twist at the top. Repeat with the remaining pastry and filling until you have 4 parcels. Brush with the remaining butter. Place the parcels on a lightly oiled baking tray and cook in the oven for 20 minutes, or until golden brown and cooked. Serve immediately.

Try This: FOR AN ALTERNATIVE: 28   FOR A SWEET TREAT: 162

Smoked Salmon Quiche

SERVES 6

225 g/8 oz plain flour
50 g/2 oz butter
50 g/2 oz white vegetable fat
or lard
2 tsp sunflower oil
225 g/8 oz potato, peeled
and diced

125 g/4 oz Gruyère cheese,
grated
75 g/3 oz smoked salmon
trimmings
5 medium eggs, beaten
300 ml/½ pint single cream
salt and freshly ground

black pepper
1 tbsp freshly chopped flat-
leaf parsley

To serve:
mixed salad
baby new potatoes

Preheat the oven to 200°C/400°F/Gas Mark 6. Blend the flour, butter and white vegetable fat or lard together until it resembles fine breadcrumbs. Blend again, adding sufficient water to make a firm but pliable dough. Use the dough to line a 23 cm/9 inch flan dish or tin, then chill the pastry case in the refrigerator for 30 minutes. Bake blind with baking beans for 10 minutes.

Heat the oil in a small frying pan, add the diced potato and cook for 3–4 minutes until lightly browned. Reduce the heat and cook for 2–3 minutes, or until tender. Leave to cool.

Scatter the grated cheese evenly over the base of the pastry case, then arrange the cooled potato on top. Add the smoked salmon in an even layer.

Beat the eggs with the cream and season to taste with salt and pepper. Whisk in the parsley and pour the mixture carefully into the dish.

Reduce the oven to 180°C/350°F/Gas Mark 4 and bake for about 30–40 minutes, or until the filling is set and golden. Serve hot or cold with a mixed salad and baby new potatoes.

Try This: FOR AN ALTERNATIVE: 34   FOR A SWEET TREAT: 248

Fish Crumble

SERVES 6

450 g/1 lb whiting or halibut
   fillets
300 ml/½ pint milk
salt and freshly ground
   black pepper
1 tbsp sunflower oil
75 g/3 oz butter or
   margarine
1 medium onion, peeled
   and finely chopped

2 leeks, trimmed and sliced
1 medium carrot, peeled and
   cut into small dice
2 medium potatoes, peeled
   and cut into small pieces
75 g/6 oz plain flour
300 ml/½ pint fish or
   vegetable stock
2 tbsp whipping cream
1 tsp freshly chopped dill

runner beans, to serve

For the crumble topping:
75 g/3 oz butter or
   margarine
175 g/6 oz plain flour
75 g/3 oz Parmesan cheese,
   grated
¾ tsp cayenne pepper

Preheat the oven to 200°C/400°F/Gas Mark 6, 15 minutes before cooking. Oil a 1.4 litre/2½ pint pie dish. Place the fish in a saucepan with the milk, salt and pepper. Bring to the boil, cover and simmer for 8–10 minutes until the fish is cooked. Remove with a slotted spoon, reserving the cooking liquid. Flake the fish into the prepared dish.

Heat the oil and 1 tablespoon of the butter or margarine in a small frying pan and gently fry the onion, leeks, carrot and potatoes for 1–2 minutes. Cover tightly and cook over a gentle heat for a further 10 minutes until softened. Spoon the vegetables over the fish.

Melt the remaining butter or margarine in a saucepan, add the flour and cook for 1 minute, stirring. Whisk in the reserved cooking liquid and the stock. Cook until thickened, then stir in the cream. Remove from the heat and stir in the dill. Pour over the fish.

To make the crumble, rub the butter or margarine into the flour until it resembles bread-crumbs, then stir in the cheese and cayenne pepper. Sprinkle over the dish, and bake in the preheated oven for 20 minutes until piping hot. Serve with runner beans.

Try This: FOR AN ALTERNATIVE: 42   FOR A SWEET TREAT: 154

Haddock with an Olive Crust

SERVES 4

12 pitted black olives,
    finely chopped
75 g/3 oz fresh white
    breadcrumbs
1 tbsp freshly
    chopped tarragon

1 garlic clove, peeled
    and crushed
3 spring onions, trimmed
    and finely chopped
1 tbsp olive oil
4 x 175 g/6 oz thick skinless

haddock fillets

To serve:
freshly cooked carrots
freshly cooked beans

Preheat the oven to 190°C/375°F/Gas Mark 5. Place the black olives in a small bowl with the breadcrumbs and add the chopped tarragon.

Add the garlic to the olives with the chopped spring onions and the olive oil. Mix together lightly.

Wipe the fillets with either a clean damp cloth or damp kitchen paper, then place on a lightly oiled baking sheet.

Place spoonfuls of the olive and breadcrumb mixture on top of each fillet and press the mixture down lightly and evenly over the top of the fish.

Bake the fish in the preheated oven for 20–25 minutes or until the fish is cooked thoroughly and the topping is golden brown. Serve immediately with the freshly cooked carrots and beans.

Try This: FOR AN ALTERNATIVE: 32   FOR A SWEET TREAT: 252

Traditional Fish Pie

SERVES 4

450 g/1 lb cod or coley fillets, skinned
450 ml/¾ pint milk
1 small onion, peeled and quartered
salt and freshly ground black pepper

900 g/2 lb potatoes, peeled and cut into chunks
100 g/3½ oz butter
125 g/4 oz large prawns
2 large eggs, hard-boiled and quartered
198 g can sweetcorn, drained

2 tbsp freshly chopped parsley
3 tbsp plain flour
50 g/2 oz Cheddar cheese, grated

Preheat the oven to 200°C/400°F/Gas Mark 6, about 15 minutes before cooking. Place the fish in a shallow frying pan, pour over 300 ml/½ pint of the milk and add the onion. Season to taste with salt and pepper. Bring to the boil and simmer for 8–10 minutes until the fish is cooked. Remove the fish with a slotted spoon and place in a 1.4 litre/2½ pint baking dish. Strain the cooking liquid and reserve.

Boil the potatoes until soft, then mash with 40 g/1½ oz of the butter and 2–3 tablespoons of the remaining milk. Reserve.

Arrange the prawns and sliced eggs on top of the fish, then scatter over the sweetcorn and sprinkle with the parsley.

Melt the remaining butter in a saucepan, stir in the flour and cook gently for 1 minute, stirring. Whisk in the reserved cooking liquid and remaining milk. Cook for 2 minutes, or until thickened, then pour over the fish mixture and cool slightly.

Spread the mashed potato over the top of the pie and sprinkle over the grated cheese. Bake in the preheated over for 30 minutes until golden. Serve immediately.

Try This: FOR AN ALTERNATIVE: 26   FOR A SWEET TREAT: 246

Saucy Cod & Pasta Bake

SERVES 4

450 g/1 lb cod fillets, skinned
2 tbsp sunflower oil
1 onion, peeled and chopped
4 rashers smoked streaky
    bacon, rind removed
    and chopped
150 g/5 oz baby button
    mushrooms, wiped
2 celery sticks, trimmed and

thinly sliced
2 small courgettes, halved
    lengthwise and sliced
400 g can chopped tomatoes
100 ml/3½ fl oz fish stock or
    dry white wine
1 tbsp freshly chopped
    tarragon
salt and freshly ground

black pepper

Pasta topping:
225–275 g/8–10 oz pasta
    shells
25 g/1 oz butter
4 tbsp plain flour
450 ml/¾ pint milk

Preheat the oven to 200°C/400°F/Gas Mark 6, 15 minutes before cooking. Cut the cod into bite-sized pieces and reserve.

Heat the sunflower oil in a large saucepan, add the onion and bacon and cook for 7–8 minutes. Add the mushrooms and celery and cook for 5 minutes, or until fairly soft. Add the courgettes and tomatoes to the bacon mixture and pour in the fish stock or wine. Bring to the boil, then simmer uncovered for 5 minutes, or until the sauce has thickened slightly. Remove from the heat and stir in the cod pieces and the tarragon. Season to taste with salt and pepper, then spoon into a large oiled baking dish.

Meanwhile, bring a large pan of lightly salted water to a rolling boil. Add the pasta shells and cook, according to the packet instructions, or until 'al dente'.

For the topping, place the butter and flour in a saucepan and pour in the milk. Bring to the boil slowly, whisking until thickened and smooth. Drain the pasta thoroughly, and stir into the sauce. Spoon carefully over the fish and vegetables. Place in the preheated oven and bake for 20–25 minutes, or until the top is lightly browned and bubbling.

Try This: FOR AN ALTERNATIVE: 42   FOR A SWEET TREAT: 240

Chilli Beef Calzone

SERVES 4

1 quantity pizza dough
   (*see* page 84)
1 tbsp sunflower oil
1 onion, peeled and

   finely chopped
1 green pepper, deseeded
   and chopped
225 g/8 oz minced beef steak

420 g can chilli beans
220 g can chopped tomatoes
mixed salad leaves, to serve

Preheat the oven to 220°C/425°F/Gas Mark 7, 15 minutes before baking. Heat the oil in a large saucepan and gently cook the onion and pepper for 5 minutes.

Add the minced beef to the saucepan and cook for 10 minutes, until browned.

Add the chilli beans and tomatoes and simmer gently for 30 minutes, or until the mince is tender. Place a baking sheet into the preheated oven to heat up.

Divide the pizza dough into 4 equal pieces. Cover 3 pieces of the dough with clingfilm and roll out the other piece on a lightly floured board to a 20.5 cm/8 inch round.

Spoon a quarter of the chilli mixture on to half of the dough round and dampen the edges with a little water.

Fold over the empty half of the dough and press the edges together well to seal.

Repeat this process with the remaining dough. Place on the hot baking sheet and bake for 15 minutes. Serve with the salad leaves.

Try This: FOR AN ALTERNATIVE: 50   FOR A SWEET TREAT: 142

Beef & Red Wine Pie

SERVES 4

1 quantity quick flaky pastry
(*see* page 92), chilled
700 g/1½ lb stewing
beef, cubed
4 tbsp seasoned plain flour
2 tbsp sunflower oil
2 onions, peeled and chopped

2 garlic cloves, peeled
and crushed
1 tbsp freshly chopped thyme
300 ml/½ pint red wine
150 ml/¼ pint beef stock
1–2 tsp Worcestershire sauce
2 tbsp tomato ketchup

2 bay leaves
a knob of butter
225 g/8 oz button mushrooms
beaten egg or milk, to glaze
sprig of parsley, to garnish

Preheat the oven to 200°C/400°F/Gas Mark 6. Toss the beef cubes in the seasoned flour.

Heat the oil in a large heavy-based frying pan. Fry the beef in batches for about 5 minutes until golden brown. Return all of the beef to the pan and add the onions, garlic and thyme. Fry for about 10 minutes, stirring occasionally. If the beef begins to stick, add a little water.

Add the red wine and stock and bring to the boil. Stir in the Worcestershire sauce, tomato ketchup and bay leaves. Cover and simmer on a very low heat for about 1 hour or until the beef is tender.

Heat the butter and gently sauté the mushrooms until golden brown. Add to the stew. Simmer uncovered for a further 15 minutes. Remove the bay leaves. Spoon the beef into a 1.1 litre/2 pint pie dish and reserve.

Roll out the pastry on a lightly floured surface. Cut out the lid to 5 mm/¼ inch wider than the dish. Brush the rim with the beaten egg and lay the pastry lid on top. Press to seal, then knock the edges with the back of the knife. Cut a slit in the lid and brush with the beaten egg or milk to glaze. Bake in the preheated oven for 30 minutes, or until golden brown. Garnish with the sprig of parsley and serve immediately.

Try This: FOR AN ALTERNATIVE: 56   FOR A SWEET TREAT: 166

Cornish Pasties

MAKES 8

For the pastry:
350 g/12 oz self-raising flour
75 g/3 oz butter or margarine
75 g/3 oz lard or white
  vegetable fat
salt and freshly ground
  black pepper

For the filling:
550 g/1¼ lb braising steak,
  chopped very finely
1 large onion, peeled and
  finely chopped
1 large potato, peeled
  and diced

200 g/7 oz swede, peeled
  and diced
3 tbsp Worcestershire sauce
1 small egg, beaten, to glaze

To garnish:
tomato slices or wedges
sprigs of fresh parsley

Preheat the oven to 180°C/350°F/Gas Mark 4, about 15 minutes before required. To make the pastry, sift the flour into a large bowl and add the fats, chopped into little pieces. Rub the fats and flour together until the mixture resembles coarse breadcrumbs. Season to taste with salt and pepper and mix again. Add about 2 tablespoons of cold water, a little at a time, and mix until the mixture comes together to form a firm but pliable dough. Turn onto a lightly floured surface, knead until smooth, then wrap and chill in the refrigerator.

To make the filling, put the braising steak in a large bowl with the onion. Add the potatoes and swede to the bowl together with the Worcestershire sauce and salt and pepper. Mix well.

Divide the dough into 8 balls and roll each ball into a circle about 25.5 cm/10 inches across. Divide the filling between the circles of pastry. Wet the edge of the pastry, then fold over the filling. Pinch the edges to seal.

Transfer the pasties to a lightly oiled baking sheet. Make a couple of small holes in each pasty and brush with beaten egg. Cook in the preheated oven for 15 minutes, remove and brush again with the egg. Return to the oven for a further 15–20 minutes until golden. Cool slightly, garnish with tomato and parsley and serve.

Try This: FOR AN ALTERNATIVE: 64   FOR A SWEET TREAT: 234

Moroccan Lamb with Apricots

SERVES 6

5 cm/2 inch piece root
    ginger, peeled and grated
3 garlic cloves, peeled and
    crushed
1 tsp ground cardamom
1 tsp ground cumin
2 tbsp olive oil

450 g/1 lb lamb neck fillet,
    cubed
1 large red onion, peeled
    and chopped
400 g can chopped tomatoes
125 g/4 oz ready-to-eat
    dried apricots

400 g can chickpeas, drained
7 large sheets filo pastry
50 g/2 oz butter, melted
pinch of nutmeg
dill sprigs, to garnish

Preheat the oven to 190°C/375°F/Gas Mark 5. Pound the ginger, garlic, cardamom and cumin to a paste with a pestle and mortar. Heat 1 tablespoon of the oil in a large frying pan and fry the spice paste for 3 minutes. Remove and reserve.

Add the remaining oil and fry the lamb in batches for about 5 minutes, until golden brown. Return all the lamb to the pan and add the onions and spice paste. Fry for 10 minutes, stirring occasionally. Add the chopped tomatoes, cover and simmer for 15 minutes. Add the apricots and chickpeas and simmer for a further 15 minutes.

Lightly oil a round 18 cm/7 inch spring form cake tin. Lay one sheet of filo pastry in the base of the tin, allowing the excess to fall over the sides. Brush with melted butter, then layer five more sheets in the tin and brush each one with butter.

Spoon in the filling and level the surface. Layer half the remaining filo sheets on top, again brushing each with butter. Fold the overhanging pastry over the top of the filling. Brush the remaining sheet with butter and scrunch up and place on top of the pie so that the whole pie is completely covered. Brush with melted butter once more. Bake in the preheated oven for 45 minutes, then reserve for 10 minutes. Unclip the tin and remove the pie. Sprinkle with the nutmeg, garnish with the dill sprigs and serve.

Try This: FOR AN ALTERNATIVE: 54   FOR A SWEET TREAT: 218

Lamb & Pasta Pie

SERVES 8

400 g/14 oz plain white flour
100 g/3½ oz margarine
100 g/3½ oz white
   vegetable fat
pinch of salt
1 small egg, separated
50 g/2 oz butter
50 g/2 oz flour

450 ml/¾ pint milk
salt and freshly ground
   black pepper
225 g/8 oz macaroni
50 g/2 oz Cheddar cheese,
   grated
1 tbsp vegetable oil
1 onion, peeled and

chopped
1 garlic clove, peeled and
   crushed
2 celery sticks, trimmed and
   chopped
450 g/1 lb lamb mince
1 tbsp tomato paste
400 g can chopped tomatoes

Preheat the oven to 190°C/375°F/Gas Mark 5, 10 minutes before cooking. Lightly oil a 20.5 cm /8 inch spring-form cake tin. Blend the flour, salt, margarine and white vegetable fat in a food processor and add cold water to make a smooth, pliable dough. Knead on a lightly floured surface, then roll out two-thirds to line the base and sides of the tin. Brush with egg white and reserve.

Melt the butter in a heavy-based pan, stir in the flour and cook for 2 minutes. Stir in the milk and cook, stirring, until a smooth, thick sauce is formed. Season to taste with salt and pepper and reserve. Bring a large pan of lightly salted water to a rolling boil. Add the macaroni and cook according to the packet instructions, or until *al dente*. Drain, then stir into the white sauce with the grated cheese. Heat the oil in a frying pan, add the onion, garlic, celery and lamb mince and cook, stirring, for 5–6 minutes. Stir in the tomato paste and tomatoes and cook for 10 minutes. Cool slightly.

Place half the pasta mixture, then all the mince in the pastry-lined tin. Top with a layer of pasta. Roll out the remaining pastry and cut out a lid. Brush the edge with water, place over the filling and pinch the edges together. Use trimmings to decorate the top of the pie. Brush the pie with beaten egg yolk and bake in the preheated oven for 50–60 minutes, covering the top with tin-foil if browning too quickly. Stand for 15 minutes before turning out. Serve immediately.

Try This: FOR AN ALTERNATIVE: 68   FOR A SWEET TREAT: 242

Shepherd's Pie

SERVES 4

2 tbsp vegetable or olive oil
1 onion, peeled and finely
  chopped
1 carrot, peeled and finely
  chopped
1 celery stalk, trimmed and
  finely chopped
1 tbsp sprigs of fresh thyme

450 g/1 lb leftover roast
  lamb, finely chopped
150 ml/¼ pint red wine
150 ml/¼ pint lamb or
  vegetable stock or
  leftover gravy
2 tbsp tomato purée
salt and freshly ground

black pepper
700 g/1½ lb potatoes, peeled
  and cut into chunks
25 g/1 oz butter
6 tbsp milk
1 tbsp freshly chopped
  parsley
fresh herbs, to garnish

Preheat the oven to 200°C/400°F/Gas Mark 6, about 15 minutes before cooking. Heat the oil in a large saucepan and add the onion, carrot and celery. Cook over a medium heat for 8–10 minutes until softened and starting to brown.

Add the thyme and cook briefly, then add the cooked lamb, wine, stock and tomato purée. Season to taste with salt and pepper and simmer gently for 25–30 minutes until reduced and thickened. Remove from the heat to cool slightly and season again.

Meanwhile, boil the potatoes in plenty of salted water for 12–15 minutes until tender. Drain and return to the saucepan over a low heat to dry out. Remove from the heat and add the butter, milk and parsley. Mash until creamy, adding a little more milk, if necessary. Adjust the seasoning.

Transfer the lamb mixture to a shallow ovenproof dish. Spoon the mash over the filling and spread evenly to cover completely. Fork the surface, place on a baking sheet, then cook in the preheated oven for 25–30 minutes until the potato topping is browned and the filling is piping hot. Garnish and serve.

Try This: FOR AN ALTERNATIVE: 52   FOR A SWEET TREAT: 254

Hot Salami & Vegetable Gratin

SERVES 4

350 g/12 oz carrots
175 g/6 oz fine green beans
250 g/9 oz asparagus tips
175 g/6 oz frozen peas
225 g/8 oz Italian salami
1 tbsp olive oil

1 tbsp freshly chopped mint
25 g/1 oz butter
150 g/5 oz baby spinach
  leaves
150 ml/¼ pint double cream
salt and freshly ground

black pepper
1 small or ½ an olive
  ciabatta loaf
75 g/3 oz Parmesan cheese,
  grated
green salad, to serve

Preheat oven to 200°C/400°F/Gas Mark 6. Peel and slice the carrots, trim the beans and asparagus and reserve. Cook the carrots in a saucepan of lightly salted, boiling water for 5 minutes. Add the remaining vegetables, except the spinach, and cook for about a further 5 minutes, or until tender. Drain and place in an ovenproof dish.

Discard any skin from the outside of the salami, if necessary, then chop roughly. Heat the oil in a frying pan and fry the salami for 4–5 minutes, stirring occasionally, until golden. Using a slotted spoon, transfer the salami to the ovenproof dish and scatter over the mint.

Add the butter to the frying pan and cook the spinach for 1–2 minutes, or until just wilted. Stir in the double cream and season well with salt and pepper. Spoon the mixture over the vegetables.

Whiz the ciabatta loaf in a food processor to make breadcrumbs. Stir in the Parmesan cheese and sprinkle over the vegetables. Bake in the preheated oven for 20 minutes, until golden and heated through. Serve with a green salad.

Try This: FOR AN ALTERNATIVE: 62   FOR A SWEET TREAT: 150

Gnocchi &
Parma Ham Bake

SERVES 4

3 tbsp olive oil
1 red onion, peeled and sliced
2 garlic cloves, peeled
175 g/6 oz plum tomatoes,
    skinned and quartered
2 tbsp sun-dried tomato paste
250 g tub mascarpone cheese

salt and freshly ground
    black pepper
1 tbsp freshly chopped
    tarragon
300 g/11 oz fresh gnocchi
125 g/4 oz Cheddar or
    Parmesan cheese, grated

50 g/2 oz fresh white
    breadcrumbs
50 g/2 oz Parma ham, sliced
10 pitted green olives, halved
sprigs of flat-leaf parsley, to
    garnish

Heat the oven to 180°C/350°F/Gas Mark 4, 10 minutes before cooking. Heat 2 tablespoons of the olive oil in a large frying pan and cook the onion and garlic for 5 minutes, or until softened. Stir in the tomatoes, sun-dried tomato paste and mascarpone cheese. Season to taste with salt and pepper. Add half the tarragon. Bring to the boil, then lower the heat immediately and simmer for 5 minutes.

Meanwhile, bring 1.7 litres/3 pints water to the boil in a large pan. Add the remaining olive oil and a good pinch of salt. Add the gnocchi and cook for 1–2 minutes, or until they rise to the surface.

Drain the gnocchi thoroughly and transfer to a large ovenproof dish. Add the tomato sauce and toss gently to coat the pasta. Combine the Cheddar or Parmesan cheese with the breadcrumbs and remaining tarragon and scatter over the pasta mixture. Top with the Parma ham and olives and season again.

Cook in the preheated oven for 20–25 minutes, or until golden and bubbling. Serve immediately, garnished with parsley sprigs.

Try This: FOR AN ALTERNATIVE: 62   FOR A SWEET TREAT: 162

Sausage & Redcurrant Pasta Bake

SERVES 4

450 g/1 lb good quality, thick pork sausages
2 tsp sunflower oil
25 g/1 oz butter
1 onion, peeled and sliced
2 tbsp plain white flour
450 ml/¾ pint chicken stock

150 ml/¼ pint port or good quality red wine
1 tbsp freshly chopped thyme leaves, plus sprigs to garnish
1 bay leaf
4 tbsp redcurrant jelly

salt and freshly ground black pepper
350 g/12 oz fresh penne
75 g/3 oz Gruyère cheese, grated

Preheat the oven to 220°C/425°F/Gas Mark 7, 15 minutes before cooking. Prick the sausages, place in a shallow ovenproof dish and toss in the sunflower oil. Cook in the oven for 25–30 minutes, or until golden brown.

Meanwhile, melt the butter in a frying pan, add the sliced onion and fry for 5 minutes, or until golden-brown. Stir in the flour and cook for 2 minutes. Remove the pan from the heat and gradually stir in the chicken stock with the port or red wine.

Return the pan to the heat and bring to the boil, stirring continuously until the sauce starts to thicken. Add the thyme, bay leaf and redcurrant jelly and season well with salt and pepper. Simmer the sauce for 5 minutes. Bring a large pan of salted water to a rolling boil, add the pasta and cook for about 4 minutes, or until 'al dente'. Drain thoroughly and reserve.

Lower the oven temperature to 200°C/400°F/Gas Mark 6. Remove the sausages from the oven, drain off any excess fat and return the sausages to the dish. Add the pasta. Pour over the sauce, removing the bay leaf, and toss together. Sprinkle with the Gruyère cheese and return to the oven for 15–20 minutes, or until bubbling and golden-brown. Serve immediately, garnished with thyme sprigs.

Try This: FOR AN ALTERNATIVE: 48   FOR A SWEET TREAT: 204

Bacon, Mushroom & Cheese Puffs

SERVES 4

1 tbsp olive oil
225 g/8 oz field mushrooms,
    wiped and roughly
    chopped
225 g/8 oz rindless streaky
    bacon, roughly chopped

2 tbsp freshly chopped parsley
salt and freshly ground
    black pepper
350 g/12 oz ready-rolled
    puff pastry sheets, thawed
    if frozen

25 g/1 oz Emmenthal
    cheese, grated
1 medium egg, beaten
salad leaves such as rocket
    or watercress, to garnish
tomatoes, to serve

Preheat the oven to 200°C/400°F/Gas Mark 6. Heat the olive oil in a large frying pan.

Add the mushrooms and bacon and fry for 6–8 minutes until golden in colour. Stir in the parsley, season to taste with salt and pepper and allow to cool.

Roll the sheet of pastry a little thinner on a lightly floured surface to a 30.5 cm/12 inch square. Cut the pastry into 4 equal squares.

Stir the grated Emmenthal cheese into the mushroom mixture. Spoon a quarter of the mixture on to one half of each square. Brush the edges of the square with a little of the beaten egg. Fold over the pastry to form a triangular parcel. Seal the edges well and place on a lightly oiled baking sheet. Repeat until the squares are done.

Make shallow slashes in the top of the pastry with a knife. Brush the parcels with the remaining beaten egg and cook in the preheated oven for 20 minutes, or until puffy and golden brown.

Serve warm or cold, garnished with the salad leaves and served with tomatoes.

Try This: FOR AN ALTERNATIVE: 50   FOR A SWEET TREAT: 230

Chicken & Ham Pie

SERVES 4

2 quantities shortcrust pastry,
(*see* page 32)
1 tbsp olive oil
1 leek, trimmed and sliced
175 g/6 oz piece of bacon,
   cut into small dice
225 g/8 oz cooked boneless

chicken meat
2 avocados, peeled, pitted
   and chopped
1 tbsp lemon juice
salt and freshly ground
   black pepper
2 large eggs, beaten

150 ml/¼ pint natural yogurt
4 tbsp chicken stock
1 tbsp poppy seeds

To serve:
sliced red onion
mixed salad leaves

Preheat the oven to 200°C/400°F/Gas Mark 6. Heat the oil in a frying pan and fry the leek and bacon for 4 minutes until soft but not coloured. Transfer to a bowl and reserve.

Cut the chicken into bite-sized pieces and add to the leek and bacon. Toss the avocado in the lemon juice, add to the chicken and season to taste with salt and pepper.

Roll out half the pastry on a lightly floured surface and use to line a 18 cm/7 inch loose- bottomed deep flan tin. Scoop the chicken mixture into the pastry case.

Mix together 1 egg, the yogurt and the chicken stock. Pour the yogurt mixture over the chicken. Roll out the remaining pastry on a lightly floured surface, and cut out the lid to 5mm/¼ inch wider than the dish.

Brush the rim with the remaining beaten egg and lay the pastry lid on top, pressing to seal. Knock the edges with the back of a knife to seal further. Cut a slit in the lid and brush with the egg.

Sprinkle with the poppy seeds and bake in the preheated oven for about 30 minutes, or until the pastry is golden brown. Serve with the onion and mixed salad leaves.

Try This: FOR AN ALTERNATIVE: 68   FOR A SWEET TREAT: 148

Sauvignon Chicken & Mushroom Filo Pie

SERVES 4

1 onion, peeled and chopped
1 leek, trimmed and chopped
225 ml/8 fl oz chicken stock
3 x 175 g/6 oz chicken breasts
150 ml/¼ pint dry white wine
1 bay leaf
175 g/6 oz baby
   button mushrooms

2 tbsp plain flour
1 tbsp freshly
   chopped tarragon
salt and freshly ground
   black pepper
sprig of fresh parsley,
   to garnish
seasonal vegetables, to serve

For the topping:
75 g/3 oz (about 5 sheets)
   filo pastry
1 tbsp sunflower oil
1 tsp sesame seeds

Preheat the oven to 190°C/375°F/Gas Mark 5. Put the onion and leek in a heavy-based saucepan with 125 ml/4 fl oz of the stock. Bring to the boil, cover and simmer for 5 minutes, then uncover and cook until all the stock has evaporated and the vegetables are tender.

Cut the chicken into bite-sized cubes. Add to the pan with the remaining stock, wine and bay leaf. Cover and gently simmer for 5 minutes. Add the mushrooms and simmer for a further 5 minutes.

Blend the flour with 3 tablespoons of cold water. Stir into the pan and cook, stirring all the time until the sauce has thickened. Stir the tarragon into the sauce and season with salt and pepper. Spoon the mixture into a 1.2 litre/2 pint pie dish, discarding the bay leaf.

Lightly brush a sheet of filo pastry with a little of the oil. Crumple the pastry slightly. Arrange on top of the filling. Repeat with the remaining filo sheets and oil, then sprinkle the top of the pie with the sesame seeds.

Bake the pie on the middle shelf of the preheated oven for 20 minutes until the filo pastry topping is golden and crisp. Garnish with a sprig of parsley. Serve the pie immediately with the seasonal vegetables.

Try This: FOR AN ALTERNATIVE: 66   FOR A SWEET TREAT: 198

Cheese & Onion Oat Pie

SERVES 4

1 tbsp sunflower oil, plus 1 tsp
25 g/1 oz butter
2 medium onions, peeled
   and sliced
1 garlic clove, peeled

  and crushed
150 g/5 oz porridge oats
125 g/4 oz mature Cheddar
  cheese, grated
2 medium eggs, lightly beaten

2 tbsp freshly chopped parsley
salt and freshly ground
  black pepper
275 g/10 oz baking potato,
  peeled

Preheat the oven to 180°C/350°F/Gas Mark 4. Heat the oil and half the butter in a saucepan until melted. Add the onions and garlic and gently cook for 10 minutes, or until soft. Remove from the heat and tip into a large bowl.

Spread the oats out on a baking sheet and toast in the hot oven for 12 minutes. Leave to cool, then add to the onions with the cheese, eggs and parsley. Season to taste with salt and pepper and mix well.

Line the base of a 20.5 cm/8 inch round sandwich tin with greaseproof paper and oil well. Thinly slice the potato and arrange the slices on the base, overlapping them slightly.

Spoon the cheese and oat mixture on top of the potato, spreading evenly with the back of a spoon. Cover with tinfoil and bake for 30 minutes.

Invert the pie onto a baking sheet so that the potatoes are on top. Carefully remove the tin and lining paper.

Preheat the grill to medium. Melt the remaining butter and carefully brush over the potato topping. Cook under the preheated grill for 5–6 minutes until the potatoes are lightly browned. Cut into wedges and serve.

Try This: FOR AN ALTERNATIVE: 60   FOR A SWEET TREAT: 168

Layered Cheese & Herb Potato Cake

SERVES 4

900 g/2 lb waxy potatoes
3 tbsp freshly snipped chives
2 tbsp freshly chopped parsley
225 g/8 oz mature Cheddar
　cheese
2 large egg yolks

1 tsp paprika
125 g/4 oz fresh white
　breadcrumbs
50 g/2 oz almonds, toasted
　and roughly chopped
50 g/2 oz butter, melted

salt and freshly ground
　black pepper
mixed salad or steamed
　vegetables, to serve

Preheat the oven to 180°C/350°F/Gas Mark 4. Lightly oil and line the base of a 20.5 cm/8 inch round cake tin with lightly oiled greaseproof or baking parchment paper. Peel and thinly slice the potatoes and reserve. Stir the chives, parsley, cheese and egg yolks together in a small bowl and reserve. Mix the paprika into the breadcrumbs.

Sprinkle the almonds over the base of the lined tin. Cover with half the potatoes, arranging them in layers, then sprinkle with the paprika bread-crumb mixture and season to taste with salt and pepper.

Spoon the cheese and herb mixture over the bread-crumbs with a little more seasoning, then arrange the remaining potatoes on top. Drizzle over the melted butter and press the surface down firmly.

Bake in the preheated oven for 1¼ hours, or until golden and cooked through. Let the tin stand for 10 minutes before carefully turning out and serving in thick wedges. Serve immediately with salad or freshly cooked vegetables.

Try This: FOR AN ALTERNATIVE: 56　FOR A SWEET TREAT: 156

Tomato & Courgette Herb Tart

SERVES 4

4 tbsp olive oil
1 onion, peeled and
  finely chopped
3 garlic cloves, peeled
  and crushed
400 g/14 oz prepared puff

pastry, thawed if frozen
1 small egg, beaten
2 tbsp freshly chopped
  rosemary
2 tbsp freshly chopped parsley
175 g/6 oz rindless fresh soft

goats' cheese
4 ripe plum tomatoes, sliced
1 medium courgette,
  trimmed and sliced
thyme sprigs, to garnish

Preheat the oven to 230°C/450°F/Gas Mark 8. Heat 2 tablespoons of the oil in a large frying pan. Fry the onion and garlic for about 4 minutes until softened and reserve.

Roll out the pastry on a lightly floured surface, and cut out a 30.5 cm/12 inch circle. Brush the pastry with a little beaten egg, then prick all over with a fork. Transfer on to a dampened baking sheet and bake in the preheated oven for 10 minutes.

Turn the pastry over and brush with a little more egg. Bake for 5 more minutes, then remove from the oven.

Mix together the onion, garlic and herbs with the goats' cheese and spread over the pastry.

Arrange the tomatoes and courgettes over the goats' cheese and drizzle with the remaining oil. Bake for 20–25 minutes, or until the pastry is golden brown and the topping bubbling. Garnish with the thyme sprigs and serve immediately.

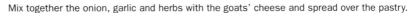

Try This: FOR AN ALTERNATIVE: 96   FOR A SWEET TREAT: 202

Potato & Goats' Cheese Tart

SERVES 6

275 g/10 oz prepared
   shortcrust pastry, thawed
   if frozen
550 g/1¼ lb small waxy
   potatoes
salt and freshly ground
   black pepper

beaten egg, for brushing
2 tbsp sun-dried tomato paste
¼ tsp chilli powder, or
   to taste
1 large egg
150 ml/¼ pint soured cream
150 ml/¼ pint milk

2 tbsp freshly snipped chives
300 g/11 oz goats' cheese,
   sliced
salad and warm crusty
   bread, to serve

Preheat the oven to 190°C/375°F/Gas Mark 5, about 10 minutes before cooking. Roll the pastry out on a lightly floured surface and use to line a 23 cm/9 inch fluted flan tin. Chill in the refrigerator for 30 minutes.

Scrub the potatoes, place in a large saucepan of lightly salted water and bring to the boil. Simmer for 10–15 minutes, or until tender. Drain and reserve until cool enough to handle.

Line the pastry case with greaseproof paper and baking beans or crumpled tinfoil and bake blind in the preheated oven for 15 minutes. Remove from the oven and discard the paper and beans or tinfoil. Brush the base with a little beaten egg, then return to the oven and cook for a further 5 minutes. Remove from the oven.

Cut the potatoes into 1 cm/½ inch thick slices; reserve. Spread the sun-dried tomato paste over the base of pastry case, sprinkle with the chilli powder, then arrange the potato slices on top in a decorative pattern.

Beat together the egg, soured cream, milk and chives, then season to taste with salt and pepper. Pour over the potatoes. Arrange the cheese on top of the potatoes. Bake in the oven for 30 minutes until golden brown and set. Serve immediately with salad and warm bread.

Try This: FOR AN ALTERNATIVE: 88   FOR A SWEET TREAT: 178

Red Pepper & Basil Tart

SERVES 4–6

For the olive pastry:
225 g/8 oz plain flour
pinch of salt
50 g/2 oz pitted black olives,
 finely chopped
1 medium egg, lightly
 beaten, plus 1 egg yolk
3 tbsp olive oil

For the filling:
2 large red peppers,
 quartered and deseeded
175 g/6 oz mascarpone
 cheese
4 tbsp milk
2 medium eggs
3 tbsp freshly chopped basil

salt and freshly ground
 black pepper
sprig of fresh basil, to
 garnish
mixed salad, to serve

Preheat oven to 200°C/400°F/Gas Mark 6, 15 minutes before cooking. Sift the flour and salt into a bowl. Make a well in the centre. Stir together the egg, oil and 1 tablespoon of tepid water. Add to the dry ingredients, drop in the olives and mix to a dough. Knead on a lightly floured surface for a few seconds until smooth, then wrap in clingfilm and chill in the refrigerator for 30 minutes.

Roll out the pastry and use to line a 23 cm/9 inch loose-bottomed fluted flan tin. Lightly prick the base with a fork. Cover and chill in the refrigerator for 20 minutes.

Cook the peppers under a hot grill for 10 minutes, or until the skins are blackened and blistered. Put the peppers in a plastic bag, cool for 10 minutes, then remove the skin and slice. Line the pastry case with tinfoil or greaseproof paper weighed down with baking beans and bake in the preheated oven for 10 minutes. Remove the tinfoil and beans and bake for a further 5 minutes. Reduce the oven temperature to 180°C/350°F/Gas Mark 4.

Beat the mascarpone cheese until smooth. Gradually add the milk and eggs. Stir in the peppers, basil and season to taste with salt and pepper. Spoon into the flan case and bake for 25–30 minutes, or until lightly set. Garnish with a sprig of fresh basil and serve with a mixed salad.

Try This: FOR AN ALTERNATIVE: 92   FOR A SWEET TREAT: 180

Three Tomato Pizza

SERVES 2–4

1 quantity pizza dough
  (*see* page 84)
3 plum tomatoes
8 cherry tomatoes
6 sun-dried tomatoes

pinch of sea salt
1 tbsp freshly chopped basil
2 tbsp extra-virgin olive oil
125 g/4 oz buffalo mozzarella
  cheese, sliced

freshly ground black pepper
fresh basil leaves, to garnish

Preheat the oven to 220°C/425°F/Gas Mark 7. Place a baking sheet into the oven to heat up.

Divide the prepared pizza dough into 4 equal pieces. Roll out one-quarter of the pizza dough on a lightly floured board to form a 20.5 cm/8 inch round. Lightly cover the 3 remaining pieces of dough with clingfilm.

Roll out the other 3 pieces into rounds, one at a time. While rolling out any piece of dough, keep the others covered with the clingfilm.

Slice the plum tomatoes, halve the cherry tomatoes and chop the sun-dried tomatoes into small pieces. Place a few pieces of each type of tomato on each pizza base then season to taste with the sea salt.

Sprinkle with the chopped basil and drizzle with the olive oil. Place a few slices of mozzarella on each pizza and season with black pepper.

Transfer the pizza on to the heated baking sheet and cook for 15–20 minutes, or until the cheese is golden brown and bubbling. Garnish with the basil leaves and serve immediately.

Try This: FOR AN ALTERNATIVE: 46   FOR A SWEET TREAT: 146

Roquefort, Parma & Rocket Pizza

SERVES 2–4

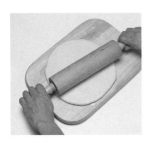

1 quantity pizza dough
  (*see* page 84)

Basic tomato sauce:
400 g can chopped tomatoes
2 garlic cloves, peeled and
  crushed
grated rind of ½ lime

2 tbsp extra-virgin olive oil
2 tbsp freshly chopped basil
½ tsp sugar
salt and freshly ground
  black pepper

For the topping:
125 g/4 oz Roquefort cheese,

cut into chunks
6 slices Parma ham
50 g/2 oz rocket leaves,
  rinsed
1 tbsp extra-virgin olive oil
50 g/2 oz Parmesan cheese,
  freshly shaved

Preheat the oven to 220°C/425°F/Gas Mark 7. Roll the pizza dough out on a lightly floured board to form a 25.5 cm/10 inch round. Lightly cover the dough and reserve while making the sauce. Place a baking sheet in the preheated oven to heat up.

Place all of the tomato sauce ingredients in a large heavy-based saucepan and slowly bring to the boil. Cover and simmer for 15 minutes, uncover and cook for a further 10 minutes until the sauce has thickened and reduced by half.

Spoon the tomato sauce over the shaped pizza dough. Place on the hot baking sheet and bake for 10 minutes.

Remove the pizza from the oven and top with the Roquefort and Parma ham, then bake for a further 10 minutes.

Toss the rocket in the olive oil and pile on to the pizza. Sprinkle with the Parmesan cheese and serve immediately.

Try This: FOR AN ALTERNATIVE: 80   FOR A SWEET TREAT: 196

Spinach, Pine Nut & Mascarpone Pizza

SERVES 2–4

Basic pizza dough:
225 g/8 oz strong plain flour
½ tsp salt
¼ tsp quick-acting dried yeast
150 ml/¼ pint warm water
1 tbsp extra-virgin olive oil

For the topping:
3 tbsp olive oil
1 large red onion, peeled and chopped
2 garlic cloves, peeled and finely sliced
450 g/1 lb frozen spinach,

thawed and drained
salt and freshly ground black pepper
3 tbsp passata
125 g/4 oz mascarpone cheese
1 tbsp toasted pine nuts

Preheat the oven to 220°C/425°F/Gas Mark 7. Sift the flour and salt into a bowl and stir in the yeast. Make a well in the centre and gradually add the water and oil to form soft dough. Knead the dough on a floured surface for about 5 minutes until smooth and elastic. Place in a lightly oiled bowl and cover with clingfilm. Leave to rise in a warm place for 1 hour.

Knock the pizza dough with your fist a few times, shape and roll out thinly on a lightly floured board. Place on a lightly floured baking sheet and lift the edge to make a little rim. Place another baking sheet into the preheated oven to heat up.

Heat half the oil in a frying pan and gently fry the onion and garlic until soft and starting to change colour.

Squeeze out any excess water from the spinach and finely chop. Add to the onion and garlic with the remaining olive oil. Season to taste with salt and pepper.

Spread the passata on the pizza dough and top with the spinach mixture. Mix the mascarpone with the pine nuts and dot over the pizza. Slide the pizza on to the hot baking sheet and bake for 15–20 minutes. Transfer to a large plate and serve immediately.

Try This: FOR AN ALTERNATIVE: 82   FOR A SWEET TREAT: 182

Stilton, Tomato & Courgette Quiche

SERVES 4

1 quantity shortcrust pastry (*see* page 32)
25 g/1 oz butter
1 onion, peeled and finely chopped

1 courgette, trimmed and sliced
125 g/4 oz Stilton cheese, crumbled
6 cherry tomatoes, halved

2 large eggs, beaten
200 ml tub crème fraîche
salt and freshly ground black pepper

Preheat the oven to 190°C/375°F/Gas Mark 5. On a lightly floured surface, roll out the pastry and use to line an 18 cm/7 inch lightly oiled quiche or flan tin, trimming any excess pastry with a knife.

Prick the base all over with a fork and bake blind in the preheated oven for 15 minutes. Remove the pastry from the oven and brush with a little of the beaten egg. Return to the oven for a further 5 minutes.

Heat the butter in a frying pan and gently fry the onion and courgette for about 4 minutes until soft and starting to brown. Transfer into the pastry case.

Sprinkle the Stilton over evenly and top with the halved cherry tomatoes. Beat together the eggs and crème fraîche and season to taste with salt and pepper.

Pour the filling into the pastry case and bake in the oven for 35–40 minutes, or until the filling is golden brown and set in the centre. Serve the quiche hot or cold.

Try This: FOR AN ALTERNATIVE: 38   FOR A SWEET TREAT: 244

Olive & Feta Parcels

MAKES 30

1 small red pepper	black olives	6 sheets filo pastry
1 small yellow pepper	125 g/4 oz feta cheese	3 tbsp olive oil
125 g/4 oz assorted	2 tbsp pine nuts, lightly	sour cream and chive dip,
marinated green and	toasted	to serve

Preheat the oven to 180°C/350°F/Gas Mark 4. Preheat the grill, then line the grill rack with tinfoil.

Cut the peppers into quarters and remove the seeds. Place skin side up on the foil-lined grill rack and cook under the preheated grill for 10 minutes, turning occasionally until the skins begin to blacken. Place the peppers in a polythene bag and leave until cool enough to handle, then skin and thinly slice.

Chop the olives and cut the feta cheese into small cubes. Mix together the olives, feta, sliced peppers and pine nuts.

Cut 1 sheet of filo pastry in half then brush with a little of the oil. Place a spoonful of the olive and feta mix about one -third of the way up the pastry. Fold over the pastry and wrap to form a square parcel encasing the filling completely.

Place this parcel in the centre of the second half of the pastry sheet. Brush the edges lightly with a little oil, bring up the corners to meet in the centre and twist them loosely to form a purse. Brush with a little more oil and repeat with the remaining filo pastry and filling.

Place the parcels on a lightly oiled baking sheet and bake in the preheated oven for 10–15 minutes, or until crisp and golden brown. Serve with the dip.

Try This: FOR AN ALTERNATIVE: 58   FOR A SWEET TREAT: 194

Fennel & Caramelised Shallot Tartlets

SERVES 6

Cheese pastry:
176 g/6 oz plain white flour
75 g/3 oz slightly salted butter
50 g/2 oz Gruyère cheese,
    grated
1 small egg yolk

For the filling:
2 tbsp olive oil
225 g/8 oz shallots, peeled
    and halved
1 fennel bulb, trimmed and
    sliced
1 tsp soft brown sugar
1 medium egg

150 ml/¼ pint double cream
salt and freshly ground
    black pepper
25 g/1 oz Gruyère cheese,
    grated
½ tsp ground cinnamon
mixed salad leaves, to serve

Preheat the oven to 200°C/400°F/Gas Mark 6. Sift the flour into a bowl, then rub in the butter, using the fingertips. Stir in the cheese, then add the egg yolk with about 2 tablespoons of cold water. Mix to a firm dough, then knead lightly. Wrap in clingfilm and chill in the refrigerator for 30 minutes.

Roll out the pastry on a lightly floured surface and use to line 6 x 10 cm/4 inch individual flan tins or patty tins which are about 2 cm/¾ inch deep.

Line the pastry cases with greaseproof paper and fill with baking beans or rice. Bake blind in the preheated oven for about 10 minutes, then remove the paper and beans.

Heat the oil in a frying pan, add the shallots and fennel and fry gently for 5 minutes. Sprinkle with the sugar and cook for a further 10 minutes, stirring occasionally until lightly caramelised. Reserve until cooled.

Beat together the egg and cream and season to taste with salt and pepper. Divide the shallot mixture between the pastry cases. Pour over the egg mixture and sprinkle with the cheese and cinnamon. Bake for 20 minutes, until golden and set. Serve with the salad leaves.

Try This: FOR AN ALTERNATIVE: 44   FOR A SWEET TREAT: 228

French Onion Tart

SERVES 4

Quick flaky pastry:
125 g/4 oz butter
175 g/6 oz plain flour
pinch of salt

For the filling:
2 tbsp olive oil
4 large onions, peeled and
   thinly sliced
3 tbsp white wine vinegar
2 tbsp muscovado sugar

a little beaten egg or milk
175 g/6 oz Cheddar
   cheese, grated
salt and freshly ground
   black pepper

Preheat the oven to 200°C/400°F/Gas Mark 6. Place the butter in the freezer for 30 minutes. Sift the flour and salt into a large bowl. Remove the butter from the freezer and grate coarsely, dipping the butter in the flour every now and again makes it easier to grate. Mix the butter into the flour, using a knife, making sure all the butter is coated thoroughly with flour.

Add 2 tablespoons of cold water and continue to mix, bringing the mixture together. Use your hands to complete the mixing. Add a little more water if needed to leave a clean bowl. Place the pastry in a polythene bag and chill in the refrigerator for 30 minutes.

Heat the oil in a large frying pan, then fry the onions for 10 minutes, stirring occasionally until softened. Stir in the vinegar and sugar. Increase the heat and stir frequently, for another 4–5 minutes until the onions turn a caramel colour. Cook for another 5 minutes, then reserve to cool.

On a lightly floured surface, roll out the pastry to a 35.5 cm/14 inch circle. Wrap over a rolling pin and move the circle on to a baking sheet. Sprinkle half the cheese over the pastry, leaving a 5 cm /2 inch border around the edge, then spoon the onions over the cheese. Fold the uncovered pastry edges over the edge of the filling to form a rim and brush the rim with beaten egg or milk.

Season to taste with salt and pepper. Sprinkle over the remaining Cheddar and bake for 20–25 minutes. Transfer to a large plate and serve immediately.

Try This: FOR AN ALTERNATIVE: 74   FOR A SWEET TREAT: 164

Parsnip Tatin

SERVES 4

1 quantity shortcrust pastry
(*see* page 32)

For the filling:
50 g/2 oz butter
8 small parsnips, peeled

and halved
1 tbsp brown sugar
75 ml/3 fl oz apple juice

Preheat the oven to 200°C/400°F/Gas Mark 6. Heat the butter in a 20.5 cm/8 inch frying pan. Add the parsnips, arranging the cut side down with the narrow ends towards the centre. Sprinkle the parsnips with sugar and cook for 15 minutes, turning halfway through until golden. Add the apple juice and bring to the boil. Remove the pan from the heat.

On a lightly floured surface, roll the pastry out to a size slightly larger than the frying pan. Position the pastry over the parsnips and press down slightly to enclose the parsnips.

Bake in the preheated oven for 20–25 minutes until the parsnips and pastry are golden.

Invert a warm serving plate over the pan and carefully turn the pan over to flip the tart on to the plate. Serve immediately.

Try This: FOR AN ALTERNATIVE: 98   FOR A SWEET TREAT: 158

Garlic Wild Mushrooms Galettes

SERVES 6

1 quantity quick flaky pastry
 (*see* page 92), chilled
1 onion, peeled
1 red chilli, deseeded
2 garlic cloves, peeled
275 g/10 oz mixed
 mushrooms e.g.

oyster, chestnuts, morels,
 ceps and chanterelles
25 g/1 oz butter
2 tbsp freshly chopped
 parsley
125 g/4 oz mozzarella
 cheese, sliced

To serve:
cherry tomatoes
mixed green salad leaves

Preheat the oven to 220°C/425°F/Gas Mark 7. On a lightly floured surface roll out the chilled pastry very thinly. Cut out 6 x 15 cm/6 inch circles and place on a lightly oiled baking sheet.

Thinly slice the onion, then divide into rings and reserve. Thinly slice the chilli and slice the garlic into wafer-thin slivers. Add to the onions and reserve.

Wipe or lightly rinse the mushrooms. Half or quarter any large mushrooms and keep the small ones whole.

Heat the butter in a frying pan and sauté the onion, chilli and garlic gently for about 3 minutes. Add the mushrooms and cook for about 5 minutes, or until beginning to soften. Stir the parsley into the mushroom mixture and drain off any excess liquid.

Pile the mushroom mixture on to the pastry circles within 5 mm/¼ inches of the edge. Arrange the sliced mozzarella cheese on top. Bake in the preheated oven for 12–15 minutes, or until golden brown and serve with the tomatoes and salad.

Try This: FOR AN ALTERNATIVE: 68   FOR A SWEET TREAT: 222

Roasted Vegetable Pie

SERVES 4

225 g/8 oz plain flour
pinch of salt
50 g/2 oz white vegetable fat
    or lard, cut into squares
50 g/2 oz butter, cut into
    squares
2 tsp herbes de Provence
1 red pepper, deseeded and
    halved

1 green pepper, deseeded
    and halved
1 yellow pepper, deseeded
    and halved
3 tbsp extra-virgin olive oil
1 aubergine, trimmed and
    sliced
1 courgette, trimmed and
    halved lengthways

1 leek, trimmed and cut
    into chunks
1 medium egg, beaten
125 g/4 oz fresh mozzarella
    cheese, sliced
salt and freshly ground
    black pepper
sprigs of mixed herbs, to
    garnish

Preheat the oven to 220°C/425°F/Gas Mark 7. Sift the flour and salt into a large bowl, add the fats and mix lightly. Using the fingertips rub into the flour until it resembles breadcrumbs. Stir in the herbes de Provence. Sprinkle over a tablespoon of cold water and with a knife start bringing the dough together. (Perhaps using the hands for the final stage.) If the dough does not form a ball instantly, add a little more water. Place in a polythene bag and chill for 30 minutes.

Place the peppers on a baking tray and sprinkle with 1 tablespoon of oil. Roast in the preheated oven for 20 minutes or until the skins start to blacken. Brush the aubergines, courgettes and leeks with oil and place on another baking tray. Roast in the oven with the peppers for 20 minutes. Place the blackened peppers in a polythene bag and leave the skin to loosen for 5 minutes. When cool enough to handle, peel the skins off the peppers.

Roll out half the pastry on a lightly floured surface and use to line a 20.5 cm/8 inch round pie dish. Line the pastry with greaseproof paper and fill with baking beans or rice and bake blind for about 10 minutes. Remove the beans and the paper, then brush the base with a little of the beaten egg. Return to the oven for 5 minutes. Layer the cooked vegetables and the cheese in the pastry case, seasoning each layer. Roll out the remaining pastry, and cut out the lid 5 mm/¼ inch wider than the dish. Brush the rim with the beaten egg and lay the pastry on top, press to seal. Knock the edges with the back of a knife. Cut a slit in the lid and brush with the beaten egg. Bake for 30 minutes. Transfer to a large serving dish, and serve immediately.

Try This: FOR AN ALTERNATIVE: 84   FOR A SWEET TREAT: 186

Breads, Scones & Teabreads

Quick Brown Bread

MAKES 2 X 450 g/1 lb LOAVES

700 g/1½ lb strong
   wholemeal flour
2 tsp salt
½ tsp caster sugar
7 g/¼ oz sachet easy-blend
   dried yeast
450 ml/¾ pint warm water

To finish:
beaten egg, to glaze
1 tbsp plain white flour,
  to dust
Onion & caraway seed rolls:
1 small onion, peeled and
  finely chopped

1 tbsp olive oil
2 tbsp caraway seeds
milk, to glaze

Preheat the oven to 200°C/400°F/Gas Mark 6, 15 minutes before baking. Oil 2 x 450 g/1 lb loaf tins. Sift the flour, salt and sugar into a large bowl, adding the remaining bran in the sieve. Stir in the yeast, then make a well in the centre. Pour the warm water into the dry ingredients and mix to form a soft dough, adding a little more water if needed.

Knead on a lightly floured surface for 10 minutes, until smooth and elastic. Divide in half, shape into 2 oblongs and place in the tins. Cover with oiled clingfilm and leave in a warm place for 40 minutes, or until risen to the top of the tins.

Glaze 1 loaf with the beaten egg and dust the other loaf generously with the plain flour. Bake the loaves in the preheated oven for 35 minutes or until well risen and lightly browned. Turn out of the tins and return to the oven for 5 minutes to crisp the sides. Cool on a wire rack.

For the onion and caraway seed rolls, gently fry the onion in the oil until soft. Reserve until the onions are cool, then stir into the dry ingredients with 1 tablespoon of the caraway seeds. Make the dough as before. Divide the dough into 16 pieces and shape into rolls. Put on 2 oiled baking trays, cover with oiled clingfilm and prove for 30 minutes. Glaze the rolls with milk and sprinkle with the rest of the seeds. Bake for 25–30 minutes, cool on a wire rack and serve.

Try This: FOR AN ALTERNATIVE: 108   FOR A SWEET TREAT: 174

Mixed Grain Bread

MAKES 1 LARGE LOAF

350 g/12 oz strong white flour
2 tsp salt
225 g/8 oz strong Granary
   flour

125 g/4 oz rye flour
25 g/1 oz butter, diced
2 tsp easy-blend dried yeast
25 g/1 oz rolled oats

2 tbsp sunflower seeds
1 tbsp malt extract
450 ml/¾ pint warm water
1 medium egg, beaten

Preheat the oven to 220°C/425°F/Gas Mark 7, 15 minutes before baking. Sift the white flour and salt into a large bowl. Stir in the Granary and rye flours, then rub in the butter until the mixture resembles breadcrumbs. Stir in the yeast, oats and seeds and make a well in the centre.

Stir the malt extract into the warm water until dissolved. Add the malt water to the dry ingredients. Mix to a soft dough. Turn the dough out on to a lightly floured surface and knead for 10 minutes, until smooth and elastic.

Put in an oiled bowl, cover with clingfilm and leave to rise in a warm place for 1½ hours or until doubled in size.

Turn out and knead again for a minute or two to knock out the air. Shape into an oval loaf about 30.5 cm/12 inches long and place on a well-oiled baking sheet. Cover with oiled clingfilm and leave to rise for 40 minutes, or until doubled in size.

Brush the loaf with beaten egg and bake in the preheated oven for 35–45 minutes, or until the bread is well risen, browned and sounds hollow when the base is tapped. Leave to cool on a wire rack, then serve.

Try This: FOR AN ALTERNATIVE: 122   FOR A SWEET TREAT: 208

Rustic Country Bread

MAKES 1 LARGE LOAF

Sourdough starter:
225 g/8 oz strong white flour
2 tsp easy-blend dried yeast
300 ml/½ pint warm water

Bread dough:
350 g/12 oz strong white flour
25 g/1 oz rye flour
1½ tsp salt
½ tsp caster sugar
1 tsp dried yeast

1 tsp sunflower oil
175 ml/6 fl oz warm water

To finish:
2 tsp plain flour
2 tsp rye flour

Preheat the oven to 220°C/425°F/Gas Mark 7, 15 minutes before baking. For the starter, sift the flour into a bowl. Stir in the yeast and make a well in the centre. Pour in the warm water and mix with a fork.

Transfer to a saucepan, cover with a clean tea towel and leave for 2–3 days at room temperature. Stir the mixture and spray with a little water twice a day.

For the dough, mix the flours, salt, sugar and yeast in a bowl. Add 225 ml/8 fl oz of the starter, the oil and the warm water. Mix to a soft dough. Knead on a lightly floured surface for 10 minutes until smooth and elastic. Put in an oiled bowl, cover and leave to rise in a warm place for about 1½ hours, or until doubled in size.

Turn the dough out and knead for a minute or two. Shape into a round loaf and place on an oiled baking sheet. Cover with oiled clingfilm and leave to rise for 1 hour, or until doubled in size.

Dust the loaf with flour, then using a sharp knife make several slashes across the top of the loaf. Slash across the loaf in the opposite direction to make a square pattern. Bake in the preheated oven for 40–45 minutes, or until golden brown and hollow sounding when tapped underneath. Cool on a wire rack and serve.

Try This: FOR AN ALTERNATIVE: 102   FOR A SWEET TREAT: 182

Classic White Loaf

MAKES 1 X 900 g/2 lb LOAF

700 g/1½ lb strong white
  flour
1 tbsp salt
25 g/1 oz butter, cubed
1 tsp caster sugar
2 tsp easy-blend dried yeast

150 ml/¼ pint milk
300 ml/½ pint warm water
1 tbsp plain flour, to dredge

Light wholemeal variation:
450 g/1 lb strong wholemeal
  flour
225 g/8 oz strong white flour
beaten egg, to glaze
1 tbsp kibbled wheat, to finish

Preheat the oven to 220°C/425°F/Gas Mark 7, 15 minutes before baking. Oil and line the base of a 900 g/2 lb loaf tin with greaseproof paper. Sift the flour and salt into a large bowl. Rub in the butter, then stir in the sugar and yeast. Make a well in the centre.

Add the milk and the warm water to the dry ingredients. Mix to a soft dough, adding a little more water if needed. Turn out the dough and knead on a lightly floured surface for 10 minutes, or until smooth and elastic.

Place the dough in an oiled bowl, cover with clingfilm or a clean tea towel and leave in a warm place to rise for 1 hour, or until doubled in size. Knead again for a minute or two to knock out the air.

Shape the dough into an oblong and place in the prepared tin. Cover with oiled clingfilm and leave to rise for a further 30 minutes or until the dough reaches the top of the tin. Dredge the top of the loaf with flour or brush with the egg glaze and scatter with kibbled wheat if making the wholemeal version. Bake the loaf on the middle shelf of the preheated oven for 15 minutes.

Turn down the oven to 200°C/400°F/Gas Mark 6. Bake the loaf for a further 20–25 minutes, or until well risen and hollow sounding when tapped underneath. Turn out, cool on a wire rack and serve.

Try This: FOR AN ALTERNATIVE: 124   FOR A SWEET TREAT: 200

Soft Dinner Rolls

MAKES 16

50 g/2 oz butter
1 tbsp caster sugar
225 ml/8 fl oz milk
550 g/1¼ lb strong white flour

1½ tsp salt
2 tsp easy-blend dried yeast
2 medium eggs, beaten

To glaze & finish:
2 tbsp milk
1 tsp sea salt
2 tsp poppy seeds

Preheat the oven to 220°C/425°F/Gas Mark 7, 15 minutes before baking. Gently heat the butter, sugar and milk in a saucepan until the butter has melted and the sugar has dissolved. Cool until tepid.

Sift the flour and salt into a bowl, stir in the yeast and make a well in the centre. Reserve 1 tablespoon of the beaten eggs. Add the rest to the dry ingredients with the milk mixture. Mix to form a soft dough.

Knead the dough on a lightly floured surface for 10 minutes until smooth and elastic. Put in an oiled bowl, cover with clingfilm and leave in a warm place to rise for 1 hour, or until doubled in size. Knead again for a minute or two, then divide into 16 pieces. Shape into plaits, snails, clover leaf and cottage buns. Place on 2 oiled baking sheets, cover with oiled clingfilm and leave to rise for 30 minutes, until doubled in size.

Mix the reserved beaten egg with the milk and brush over the rolls. Sprinkle some with sea salt, others with poppy seeds and leave some plain. Bake in the preheated oven for about 20 minutes, or until golden and hollow sounding when tapped underneath. Transfer to a wire rack. Cover with a clean tea towel while cooling to keep the rolls soft and serve.

Try This: FOR AN ALTERNATIVE: 138   FOR A SWEET TREAT: 214

Bagels

SERVES 4

450 g/1 lb strong plain flour
1½ tsp salt
2 tsp easy-blend dried yeast
2 medium eggs
1 tsp clear honey

2 tbsp sunflower oil
250 ml/9 fl oz tepid water

To finish:
1 tbsp caster sugar

beaten egg, to glaze
2 tsp poppy seeds
½ small onion, peeled and
    finely chopped
2 tsp sunflower oil

Preheat the oven to 200°C/400°F/Gas Mark 6, 15 minutes before baking. Sift the flour and salt into a large bowl. Stir in the yeast, then make a well in the centre. Whisk the eggs together with the honey and oil. Add to the dry ingredients with the tepid water and mix to form a soft dough.

Knead the dough on a lightly floured surface for 10 minutes until smooth and elastic. Put in a bowl, cover with clingfilm and leave in a warm place to rise for 45 minutes, or until doubled in size.

Briefly knead the dough again to knock out the air. Divide into 12 pieces, form each into a 20.5 cm /8 inch roll, curve into a ring and pinch the edges to seal.

Put the rings on an oiled baking sheet, cover with oiled clingfilm and leave to rise in a warm place for 20 minutes, or until risen and puffy.

Add the caster sugar to a large saucepan of water. Bring to the boil, then drop in the bagels, one at a time and poach for 15 seconds. Lift out with a slotted spoon and return to the baking tray.

Brush the bagels with beaten egg and sprinkle one-third with poppy seeds. Mix together the onion and oil and sprinkle over another third of the bagels. Leave the remaining third plain.

Bake in the preheated oven for 12–15 minutes, or until golden brown. Transfer to a wire rack and serve when cool.

Try This: FOR AN ALTERNATIVE: 122   FOR A SWEET TREAT: 170

Irish Soda Bread

MAKES 1 LOAF

400 g/14 oz plain white flour,
plus 1 tbsp for dusting
1 tsp salt
2 tsp bicarbonate of soda
15 g/½ oz butter

50 g/2 oz coarse oatmeal
1 tsp clear honey
300 ml/½ pint buttermilk
2 tbsp milk

Wholemeal variation:
400 g/14 oz plain wholemeal
flour, plus 1 tbsp for
dusting
1 tbsp milk

Preheat the oven to 200°C/400°F/Gas Mark 6, 15 minutes before baking. Sift the flour, salt and bicarbonate of soda into a large bowl. Rub in the butter until the mixture resembles fine breadcrumbs. Stir in the oatmeal and make a well in the centre.

Mix the honey, buttermilk and milk together and add to the dry ingredients. Mix to a soft dough.

Knead the dough on a lightly floured surface for 2–3 minutes, until the dough is smooth. Shape into a 20.5 cm/8 inch round and place on an oiled baking sheet.

Thickly dust the top of the bread with flour. Using a sharp knife, cut a deep cross on top, going about halfway through the loaf.

Bake in the preheated oven on the middle shelf of the oven for 30–35 minutes or until the bread is slightly risen, golden and sounds hollow when tapped underneath. Cool on a wire rack. Eat on the day of making.

For a wholemeal soda bread, use all the wholemeal flour instead of the white flour and add an extra tablespoon of milk when mixing together. Dust the top with wholemeal flour and bake.

Try This: FOR AN ALTERNATIVE: 128   FOR A SWEET TREAT: 144

Spicy Filled Naan Bread

MAKES 6

400 g/14 oz strong white flour
1 tsp salt
1 tsp easy-blend dried yeast
15 g/½ oz ghee or unsalted
    butter, melted
1 tsp clear honey
200 ml/7 fl oz warm water

For the filling:
25 g/1 oz ghee or unsalted
    butter
1 small onion, peeled and
    finely chopped
1 garlic clove, peeled
    and crushed

1 tsp ground coriander
1 tsp ground cumin
2 tsp grated fresh root ginger
pinch of chilli powder
pinch of ground cinnamon
salt and freshly ground
    black pepper

Preheat the oven to 220°C/450°F/Gas Mark 8, 15 minutes before baking and place a large baking sheet in to heat up. Sift the flour and salt into a large bowl. Stir in the yeast and make a well in the centre. Add the ghee or melted butter, honey and the warm water. Mix to a soft dough. Knead the dough on a lightly floured surface, until smooth and elastic. Put in a lightly oiled bowl, cover with clingfilm and leave to rise for 1 hour, or until doubled in size.

For the filling, melt the ghee or butter in a frying pan and gently cook the onion for about 5 minutes. Stir in the garlic and spices and season to taste with salt and pepper. Cook for a further 6–7 minutes, until soft. Remove from the heat, stir in 1 tablespoon of water and leave to cool.

Briefly knead the dough, then divide into 6 pieces. Roll out each piece of dough to 12.5 cm/ 5 inch rounds. Spoon the filling on to one half of each round.

Fold over and press the edges together to seal. Re-roll to shape into flat ovals, about 16 cm/6½ inches long. Cover with oiled clingfilm and leave to rise for about 15 minutes.

Transfer the breads to the hot baking sheet and cook in the preheated oven for 10–12 minutes, until puffed up and lightly browned. Serve hot.

Try This: FOR AN ALTERNATIVE: 122   FOR A SWEET TREAT: 216

Bacon & Tomato Breakfast Twist

SERVES 8

450 g/1 lb strong plain flour
½ tsp salt
7 g/¼ oz sachet easy-blend
    dried yeast
300 ml/½ pint warm milk
15 g/½ oz butter, melted

For the filling:
225 g/8 oz back bacon,
    derinded
15 g/½ oz butter, melted
175 g/6 oz ripe tomatoes,
    peeled, deseeded

and chopped
freshly ground black pepper

To finish:
beaten egg, to glaze
2 tsp medium oatmeal

Preheat the oven to 200°C/400°F/Gas Mark 6, 15 minutes before baking. Sift the flour and salt into a large bowl. Stir in the yeast and make a well in the centre. Pour in the milk and butter and mix to a soft dough. Knead on a lightly floured surface for 10 minutes, until smooth and elastic. Put in an oiled bowl, cover with clingfilm and leave to rise in a warm place for 1 hour, until doubled in size.

Cook the bacon under a hot grill for 5–6 minutes, turning once until crisp. Once cool, chop roughly.

Knead the dough again for a minute or two. Roll it out to a 25.5 x 33 cm/10 x 13 inch rectangle. Cut in half lengthways. Lightly brush with butter, then scatter with the bacon, tomatoes and black pepper, leaving a 1 cm/ ½ inch margin around the edges. Brush the edges of the dough with beaten egg, then roll up each rectangle lengthways.

Place the 2 rolls side by side and twist together, pinching the ends to seal. Transfer to an oiled baking sheet and loosely cover with oiled clingfilm. Leave to rise in a warm place for 30 minutes.

Brush with the beaten egg and sprinkle with the oatmeal. Bake in the preheated oven for about 30 minutes, or until golden brown and hollow sounding when tapped on the base. Serve the bread warm in thick slices.

Try This: FOR AN ALTERNATIVE: 106   FOR A SWEET TREAT: 220

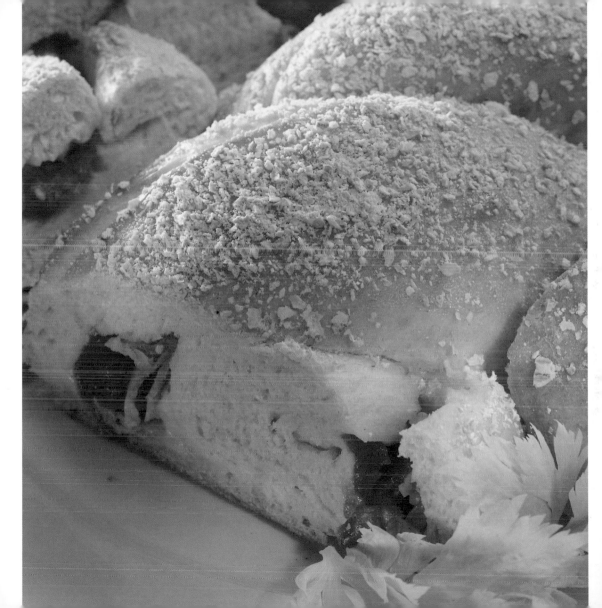

Rosemary & Olive Focaccia

MAKES 2 LOAVES

700 g/1½ lb strong white flour
pinch of salt
pinch of caster sugar
7 g/¼ oz sachet easy-blend
   dried yeast
2 tsp freshly chopped
   rosemary

450 ml/¾ pint warm water
3 tbsp olive oil
75 g/3 oz pitted black olives,
   roughly chopped
sprigs of rosemary, to garnish

To finish:
3 tbsp olive oil
coarse sea salt
freshly ground black pepper

Preheat the oven to 200°C/400°F/Gas Mark 6, 15 minutes before baking. Sift the flour, salt and sugar into a large bowl. Stir in the yeast and rosemary. Make a well in the centre.

Pour in the warm water and the oil and mix to a soft dough. Turn out on to a lightly floured surface and knead for about 10 minutes, until smooth and elastic.

Pat the olives dry on kitchen paper, then gently knead into the dough. Put in an oiled bowl, cover with clingfilm and leave to rise in a warm place for 1½ hours, or until it has doubled in size.

Turn out the dough and knead again for a minute or two. Divide in half and roll out each piece to a 25.5 cm/10 inch circle. Transfer to oiled baking sheets, cover with oiled clingfilm and leave to rise for 30 minutes.

Using the fingertips, make deep dimples all over the the dough. Drizzle with the oil and sprinkle with sea salt.

Bake in the preheated oven for 20–25 minutes, or until risen and golden. Cool on a wire rack and garnish with sprigs of rosemary. Grind over a little black pepper before serving.

Try This: FOR AN ALTERNATIVE: 126   FOR A SWEET TREAT: 334

Sweet Potato Baps

MAKES 16

225 g/8 oz sweet potato
15 g/½ oz butter
freshly grated nutmeg
about 200 ml/7 fl oz milk
450 g/1 lb strong white flour

2 tsp salt
7 g/¼ oz sachet easy-blend
  yeast
1 medium egg, beaten

To finish:
beaten egg, to glaze
1 tbsp rolled oats

Preheat the oven to 200°C/400°F/Gas Mark 6, 15 minutes before baking. Peel the sweet potato and cut into large chunks. Cook in a saucepan of boiling water for 12–15 minutes, or until tender. Drain well and mash with the butter and nutmeg. Stir in the milk, then leave until barely warm.

Sift the flour and salt into a large bowl. Stir in the yeast. Make a well in the centre. Add the mashed sweet potato and beaten egg and mix to a soft dough. Add a little more milk if needed, depending on the moisture in the sweet potato.

Turn out the dough on to a lightly floured surface and knead for about 10 minutes, or until smooth and elastic. Place in a lightly oiled bowl, cover with clingfilm and leave in a warm place to rise for about 1 hour, or until the dough doubles in size.

Turn out the dough and knead for a minute or two until smooth. Divide into 16 pieces, shape into rolls and place on a large oiled baking sheet. Cover with oiled clingfilm and leave to rise for 15 minutes. Brush the rolls with beaten egg, then sprinkle half with rolled oats and leave the rest plain.

Bake in the preheated oven for 12–15 minutes, or until well risen, lightly browned and sound hollow when the bases are tapped. Transfer to a wire rack and immediately cover with a clean tea towel to keep the crusts soft.

Try This: FOR AN ALTERNATIVE: 130   FOR A SWEET TREAT: 260

Cheese–crusted Potato Scones

MAKES 6

200 g/7 oz self-raising flour
25 g/1 oz wholemeal flour
½ tsp salt
1½ tsp baking powder
25 g/1 oz butter, cubed
5 tbsp milk

175 g/6 oz cold mashed
    potato
freshly ground black pepper

To finish:
2 tbsp milk

40 g/1½ oz mature Cheddar
    cheese, finely grated
paprika pepper, to dust
sprig of basil, to garnish

Preheat the oven to 220°C/425°F/Gas Mark 7, 15 minutes before baking. Sift the flours, salt and baking powder into a large bowl. Rub in the butter until the mixture resembles fine breadcrumbs.

Stir 4 tablespoons of the milk into the mashed potato and season with black pepper. Add the dry ingredients to the potato mixture, mixing together with a fork and adding the remaining 1 tablespoon of milk if needed.

Knead the dough on a lightly floured surface for a few seconds until smooth. Roll out to a 15 cm /6 inch round and transfer to an oiled baking sheet.

Mark the scone round into 6 wedges, cutting about halfway through with a small sharp knife.

Brush with milk, then sprinkle with the cheese and a faint dusting of paprika. Bake on the middle shelf of the preheated oven for 15 minutes, or until well risen and golden brown.

Transfer to a wire rack and leave to cool for 5 minutes before breaking into wedges. Serve warm or leave to cool completely. Once cool store the scones in an airtight tin. Garnish with a sprig of basil and serve split and buttered.

Try This: FOR AN ALTERNATIVE: 118   FOR A SWEET TREAT: 176

Traditional Oven Scones

MAKES 8

225 g/8 oz self-raising flour
1 tsp baking powder
pinch of salt
40 g/1½ oz butter, cubed
15 g/½ oz caster sugar

150 ml/¼ pint milk, plus
1 tbsp for brushing
1 tbsp plain flour, to dust

**Lemon & sultana
scone variation:**
50 g/2 oz sultanas
finely grated rind of ½ lemon
beaten egg, to glaze

Preheat the oven to 220°C/425°F/Gas Mark 7, 15 minutes before baking. Sift the flour, baking powder and salt into a large bowl. Rub in the butter until the mixture resembles fine breadcrumbs. Stir in the sugar and mix in enough milk to give a fairly soft dough.

Knead the dough on a lightly floured surface for a few seconds until smooth. Roll out until 2 cm/¾ inches thick and stamp out 6.5 cm/2½ inch rounds with a floured plain cutter.

Place on an oiled baking sheet and brush the tops with milk (do not brush it over the sides or the scones will not rise properly). Dust with a little plain flour.

Bake in the preheated oven for 12–15 minutes, or until well risen and golden brown. Transfer to a wire rack and serve warm or leave to cool completely. (The scones are best eaten on the day of baking but may be kept in an airtight tin for up to 2 days.)

For lemon and sultana scones, stir in the sultanas and lemon rind with the sugar. Roll out until 2 cm/¾ inches thick and cut into 8 fingers, 10 x 2.5 cm/4 x 1 inch in size. Bake the scones as before.

Try This: FOR AN ALTERNATIVE: 104   FOR A SWEET TREAT: 192

Daktyla–style Bread

MAKES 1 LOAF

350 g/12 oz strong white
  flour
125 g/4 oz wholemeal flour
1 tsp salt
50 g/2 oz fine cornmeal

2 tsp easy-blend dried yeast
2 tsp clear honey
1 tbsp olive oil
4 tbsp milk
250 ml/9 fl oz water

To glaze & finish:
4 tbsp milk
4 tbsp sesame seeds

Preheat the oven to 220˚C/425˚F/Gas Mark 7, 15 minutes before baking. Sift the white and wholemeal flours and salt into a large bowl, adding the bran left in the sieve. Stir in the cornmeal and yeast. Make a well in the centre.

Put the honey, oil, milk and water in a saucepan and heat gently until tepid. Add to the dry ingredients and mix to a soft dough, adding a little more water if needed.

Knead the dough on a lightly floured surface for 10 minutes, until smooth and elastic. Put in an oiled bowl, cover with clingfilm and leave to rise in a warm place for 1½ hours or until it has doubled in size.

Turn the dough out and knead for a minute or two. Shape into a long oval about 25.5 cm/10 inches long. Cut the oval into 6 equal pieces. Shape each piece into an oblong, then on an oiled baking sheet arrange in a row so that all the pieces of dough are touching. Cover with oiled clingfilm and leave for 45 minutes, or until doubled in size.

Brush the bread with milk, then scatter with sesame seeds. Bake the bread in the preheated oven for 40–45 minutes, or until golden brown and hollow sounding when tapped underneath. Cool on a wire rack and serve.

Try This: FOR AN ALTERNATIVE: 102   FOR A SWEET TREAT: 218

Moist Mincemeat Tea Loaf

CUTS INTO 12 SLICES

225 g/8 oz self-raising flour
½ tsp ground mixed spice
125 g/4 oz cold butter, cubed
75 g/3 oz flaked almonds
25 g/1 oz glacé cherries,

rinsed, dried and quartered
75 g/3 oz light muscovado sugar
2 medium eggs
250 g/9 oz prepared

mincemeat
1 tsp lemon zest
2 tsp brandy or milk

Preheat the oven to 180°C/350°F/Gas Mark 4, 10 minutes before cooking. Oil and line the base of a 900 g/2 lb loaf tin with non-stick baking paper.

Sift the flour and mixed spice into a large bowl. Add the butter and rub in until the mixture resembles breadcrumbs. Reserve 2 tablespoons of the flaked almonds and stir in the rest with the glacé cherries and sugar.

Make a well in the centre of the dry ingredients. Lightly whisk the eggs, then stir in the mincemeat, lemon zest and brandy or milk.

Add the egg mixture and fold together until blended. Spoon into the prepared loaf tin, smooth the top with the back of a spoon, then sprinkle over the reserved flaked almonds.

Bake on the middle shelf of the preheated oven for 30 minutes. Cover with tinfoil to prevent the almonds browning too much. Bake for a further 30 minutes, or until well risen and a skewer inserted into the centre comes out clean.

Leave the tea loaf in the tin for 10 minutes before removing and cooling on a wire rack. Remove the lining paper, slice thickly and serve.

Try This: FOR AN ALTERNATIVE: 134   FOR A SWEET TREAT: 184

Spiced Apple Doughnuts

MAKES 8

225 g/8 oz strong white flour
½ tsp salt
1½ tsp ground cinnamon
1 tsp easy-blend dried yeast
75 ml/3 fl oz warm milk

25 g/1 oz butter, melted
1 medium egg, beaten
oil, to deep-fry
4 tbsp caster sugar, to coat

For the filling:
2 small eating apples, peeled,
    cored and chopped
2 tsp soft light brown sugar
2 tsp lemon juice

Sift the flour, salt and 1 teaspoon of the cinnamon into a large bowl. Stir in the yeast and make a well in the centre. Add the milk, butter and egg and mix to a soft dough. Knead on a lightly floured surface for 10 minutes, until smooth and elastic.

Divide the dough into 8 pieces and shape each into a ball. Put on a floured baking sheet, cover with oiled clingfilm and leave in a warm place for 1 hour, or until doubled in size.

To make the filling, put the apples in a saucepan with the sugar, lemon juice and 3 tablespoons of water. Cover and simmer for about 10 minutes, then uncover and cook until fairly dry, stirring occasionally. Mash or blend in a food processor to a purée.

Pour enough oil into a deep-fat frying pan to come one-third of the way up the pan. Heat the oil to 180°C/350°F, then deep-fry the doughnuts for 1½–2 minutes on each side, until well browned.

Drain the doughnuts on kitchen paper, then roll in the caster sugar mixed with the remaining ½ teaspoon of ground cinnamon. Push a thick skewer into the centre to make a hole, then pipe in the apple filling. Serve warm or cold.

Fruity Apple Tea Bread

CUTS INTO 12 SLICES

125 g/4 oz butter
125 g/4 oz soft light
   brown sugar
275 g/10 oz sultanas
150 ml/¼ pint apple juice
1 eating apple, peeled cored
   and chopped

2 medium eggs, beaten
275 g/10 oz plain flour
½ tsp ground cinnamon
½ tsp ground ginger

To decorate:
1 eating apple, cored

and sliced
2 tsp bicarbonate of soda
curls of butter, to serve
1 tsp lemon juice
1 tbsp golden syrup, warmed

Preheat the oven to 180°C/350°F/Gas Mark 4. Oil and line the base of a 900 g/2 lb loaf tin with non-stick baking paper.

Put the butter, sugar, sultanas and apple juice in a small saucepan. Heat gently, stirring occasionally until the butter has melted. Tip into a bowl and leave to cool. Stir in the chopped apple and beaten eggs. Sift the flour, spices and bicarbonate of soda over the apple mixture. Stir into the sultana mixture, spoon into the prepared loaf tin and smooth the top level with the back of a spoon.

Toss the apple slices in lemon juice and arrange on top. Bake in the preheated oven for 50 minutes. Cover with tinfoil to prevent the top from browning too much.

Bake for 30–35 minutes, or until a skewer inserted into the centre comes out clean.

Leave in the tin for 10 minutes before turning out to cool on to a wire rack. Brush the top with golden syrup and leave to cool. Remove the lining paper, cut into thick slices and serve with curls of butter.

Try This: FOR AN ALTERNATIVE: 136 FOR A SWEET TREAT: 244

Fruited Brioche Buns

MAKES 12

225 g/8 oz strong white flour
pinch of salt
1 tbsp caster sugar
7 g/¼ oz sachet easy-blend
   dried yeast
2 large eggs, beaten

50 g/2 oz butter, melted
beaten egg, to glaze

For the filling:
40 g/1½ oz blanched
   almonds, chopped

50 g/2 oz luxury mixed
   dried fruit
1 tsp light soft brown sugar
2 tsp orange liqueur or
   brandy

Preheat the oven to 220°C/425°F/Gas Mark 7, 15 minutes before baking. Sift the flour and salt into a bowl. Stir in the sugar and yeast. Make a well in the centre. Add the eggs, butter and 2 tablespoons of warm water and mix to a soft dough.

Knead the dough on a floured surface for 5 minutes, until smooth and elastic. Put in an oiled bowl, cover with clingfilm and leave to rise in a warm place for 1 hour, or until it has doubled in size.

Mix the filling ingredients together, cover the bowl and leave to soak while the dough is rising.

Re-knead the dough for a minute or two, then divide into 12 pieces. Take 1 piece at a time and flatten three-quarters into a 6.5 cm/2½ inch round. Spoon a little filling in the centre, then pinch the edges together to enclose. Put seam-side down into a well-greased fluted 12-hole bun tin.

Shape the smaller piece of dough into a round and place on top of the larger one. Push a finger or floured wooden spoon handle through the middle of the top one and into the bottom one to join them together. Repeat with the remaining balls of dough. Cover the brioche with oiled clingfilm and leave for about 20 minutes, or until well risen.

Brush the brioches with beaten egg and bake in the preheated oven for 10–12 minutes, or until golden. Cool on a wire rack and serve.

Try This: FOR AN ALTERNATIVE: 104   FOR A SWEET TREAT: 214

Maple, Pecan & Lemon Loaf

CUTS INTO 12 SLICES

350 g/12 oz plain flour
1 tsp baking powder
175 g/6 oz butter, cubed
75 g/3 oz caster sugar
125 g/4 oz pecan nuts,

roughly chopped
3 medium eggs
1 tbsp milk
finely grated rind of 1 lemon
5 tbsp maple syrup

For the icing:
75 g/3 oz icing sugar
1 tbsp lemon juice
25 g/1 oz pecans,
   roughly chopped

Preheat the oven to 170°C/325°F/Gas Mark 3, 10 minutes before baking. Lightly oil and line the base of a 900 g/2 lb loaf tin with non-stick baking parchment.

Sift the flour and baking powder into a large bowl. Rub in the butter until the mixture resembles fine breadcrumbs. Stir in the caster sugar and pecan nuts.

Beat the eggs together with the milk and lemon rind. Stir in the maple syrup. Add to the dry ingredients and gently stir in until mixed thoroughly to make a soft dropping consistency.

Spoon the mixture into the prepared tin and level the top with the back of a spoon. Bake on the middle shelf of the preheated oven for 50–60 minutes, or until the cake is well risen and lightly browned. If a skewer inserted into the centre comes out clean, then the cake is ready.

Leave the cake in the tin for about 10 minutes, then turn out and leave to cool on a wire rack. Carefully remove the lining paper.

Sift the icing sugar into a small bowl and stir in the lemon juice to make a smooth icing. Drizzle the icing over the top of the loaf, then scatter with the chopped pecans. Leave to set, thickly slice and serve.

Try This: FOR AN ALTERNATIVE: 110   FOR A SWEET TREAT: 256

Baked Puddings, Sweet Tarts & Pies

Orange Curd & Plum Puddings

SERVES 4

700 g/1½ lb plums, stoned
and quartered
2 tbsp light brown sugar
grated rind of ½ lemon
25 g/1 oz butter, melted

1 tbsp olive oil
6 sheets filo pastry
½ x 411 g jar luxury
orange curd
50 g/2 oz sultanas

icing sugar, to decorate
half-fat thick set Greek
yogurt, to serve

Preheat the oven to 200°C/400° F/Gas Mark 6. Lightly oil a 20.5 cm/8 inch round cake tin. Cook the plums with 2 tablespoons of the light brown sugar for 8–10 minutes to soften them, remove from the heat and reserve.

Mix together the lemon rind, butter and oil. Lay a sheet of pastry in the prepared cake tin and brush with the lemon rind mixture.

Cut the sheets of filo pastry in half and then place one half sheet in the cake tin and brush again.

Top with the remaining halved sheets of pastry brushing each time with the lemon rind mixture. Fold each sheet in half lengthwise to line the sides of the tin to make a filo case.

Mix together the plums, orange curd and sultanas and spoon into the pastry case.

Draw the pastry edges up over the filling to enclose. Brush the remaining sheets of filo pastry with the lemon rind mixture and cut into thick strips.

Scrunch each strip of pastry and arrange on top of the pie. Bake in the preheated oven for 25 minutes, until golden. Sprinkle with icing sugar and serve with the Greek yogurt.

Try This: FOR AN ALTERNATIVE: 152 FOR A SAVOURY OPTION: 24

Topsy Turvy Pudding

SERVES 6

For the topping:
175 g/6 oz demerara sugar
2 oranges

For the sponge:
175 g/6 oz butter, softened

175 g/6 oz caster sugar
3 medium eggs, beaten
175 g/6 oz self-raising flour,
 sifted
50 g/2 oz plain dark
 chocolate, melted

grated rind of 1 orange
25 g/1 oz cocoa powder,
 sifted
custard or soured cream,
 to serve

Preheat the oven to 180°C/350°F/Gas Mark 4, 10 minutes before baking. Lightly oil a 20.5 cm/8 inch deep round loose-based cake tin. Place the demerara sugar and 3 tablespoons of water in a small heavy-based saucepan and heat gently until the sugar has dissolved. Swirl the saucepan or stir with a clean wooden spoon to ensure the sugar has dissolved, then bring to the boil and boil rapidly until a golden caramel is formed. Pour into the base of the tin and leave to cool.

For the sponge, cream the butter and sugar together until light and fluffy. Gradually beat in the eggs a little at a time, beating well between each addition. Add a spoonful of flour after each addition to prevent the mixture curdling. Add the melted chocolate and then stir well. Fold in the orange rind, self-raising flour and sifted cocoa powder and mix well.

Remove the peel from both oranges taking care to remove as much of the pith as possible. Thinly slice the peel into strips and then slice the oranges. Arrange the peel and then the orange slices over the caramel. Top with the sponge mixture and level the top.

Place the tin on a baking sheet and bake in the preheated oven for 40–45 minutes or until well risen, golden brown and an inserted skewer comes out clean. Remove from the oven, leave for about 5 minutes, invert onto a serving plate and sprinkle with cocoa powder. Serve with either custard or soured cream.

Try This: FOR AN ALTERNATIVE: 158   FOR A SAVOURY OPTION: 48

Rice Pudding

SERVES 4

60 g/2½ oz pudding rice
50 g/2 oz granulated sugar
410 g can light
    evaporated milk

300 ml/½ pint semi-
    skimmed milk
pinch of freshly
    grated nutmeg

25 g/1 oz half-fat butter
reduced sugar jam,
    to decorate

Preheat the oven to 150°C/300°F/Gas Mark 2. Lightly oil a large ovenproof dish. Sprinkle the rice and the sugar into the dish and mix.

Bring the evaporated milk and milk to the boil in a small pan, stirring occasionally. Stir the milks into the rice and mix well until the rice is coated thoroughly.

Sprinkle over the nutmeg, cover with tinfoil and bake in the preheated oven for 30 minutes.

Remove the pudding from the oven and stir well, breaking up any lumps.

Cover with the same tinfoil. Bake in the preheated oven for a further 30 minutes. Remove from the oven and stir well again.

Dot the pudding with butter and bake for a further 45–60 minutes, until the rice is tender and the skin is browned.

Divide the pudding into 4 individual serving bowls. Top with a large spoonful of the jam and serve immediately.

Try This: FOR AN ALTERNATIVE: 156 FOR A SAVOURY OPTION: 52

Lemon Surprise

SERVES 4

75 g /3 oz half-fat margarine
175 g/6 oz caster sugar
3 medium eggs, separated
75 g/3 oz self-raising flour

450 ml/¾ pint semi-
    skimmed milk
juice of 2 lemons
juice of 1 orange

2 tsp icing sugar
lemon twists, to decorate
sliced strawberries, to serve

Preheat the oven to 190°C/375°F/Gas Mark 5. Lightly oil a deep ovenproof dish.

Beat together the margarine and sugar until pale and fluffy.

Add the egg yolks, one at a time, with 1 tablespoon of the flour and beat well after each
addition. Once added, stir in the remaining flour. Stir in the milk, 4 tablespoons of the lemon
juice and 3 tablespoons of the orange juice.

Whisk the egg whites until stiff and fold into the pudding mixture with a metal spoon or rubber
spatula until well combined. Pour into the prepared dish.

Stand the dish in a roasting tin and pour in just enough boiling water to come halfway up the
sides of the dish.

Bake in the preheated oven for 45 minutes, until well risen and spongy to the touch.

Remove the pudding from the oven and sprinkle with the icing sugar. Decorate with the lemon
twists and serve immediately with the strawberries.

Try This: FOR AN ALTERNATIVE: 226 FOR A SAVOURY OPTION: 90

'Mars' Bar Mousse in Filo Cups

SERVES 6

6 large sheets filo pastry,
thawed if frozen
40 g/1½ oz unsalted butter,
melted
1 tbsp caster sugar
3 x 60 g/2½ oz 'Mars' bars,
coarsely chopped

1½ tbsp milk
300 ml/½ pint double cream
1 large egg white
1 tsp cocoa powder
1 tbsp plain dark grated
chocolate
chocolate sauce, to

serve (optional)

For topping:
300 ml/½ pint whipping cream
125 g/4 oz white chocolate,
grated
1 tsp vanilla essence

Preheat the oven to 180°C/350°F/Gas Mark 4, 10 minutes before baking. Lightly oil 6 x 150 ml/¼ pint ramekins. Cut the filo pastry into 15 cm/6 inch squares, place 1 square on the work surface, then brush with a little of the melted butter, sprinkle with a little caster sugar. Butter a second square and lay it over the first at an angle, sprinkle with a little more caster sugar and repeat with 2 more pastry squares.

Press the assembled filo pastry into the oiled ramekin, pressing into the base to make a flat bottom and keeping the edges pointing up. Continue making the cups in this way, then place on a baking sheet and bake in the preheated oven for 10–15 minutes or until crisp and golden. Remove and leave to cool before removing the filo cups from the ramekins. Leave until cold.

Melt the 'Mars' bars and milk in a small saucepan, stirring constantly until melted and smooth. Leave to cool for 10 minutes, stirring occasionally. Whisk the cream until thick and stir a spoonful into the melted 'Mars' bar mixture, then fold in the remaining cream. Whisk the egg white until stiff and fold into the 'Mars' bar mixture together with the cocoa powder. Chill the mousse in the refrigerator for 2–3 hours. For the topping, boil 125 ml/4 fl oz of the whipping cream, add the grated white chocolate and vanilla essence and stir until smooth, then strain into a bowl and leave to cool. Whisk the remaining cream until thick, then fold into the white chocolate cream mixture. Spoon the mousse into the filo cups, cover with the cream mixture and sprinkle with grated chocolate. Chill in the refrigerator before serving with chocolate sauce, if liked.

Try This: FOR AN ALTERNATIVE: 336 FOR A SAVOURY OPTION: 62

Cherry Batter Pudding

SERVES 4

450 g/1 lb fresh cherries (or
    425 g can pitted cherries)
50 g/2 oz plain flour
pinch of salt

3 tbsp caster sugar
2 medium eggs
300 ml/½ pint milk
40 g/1½ oz butter

1 tbsp rum
extra caster sugar, to dredge
fresh cream, to serve

Preheat the oven to 220°C/425°F/Gas Mark 7. Lightly oil a 900 ml/1½ pint shallow baking dish.

Rinse the cherries, drain well and remove the stones (using a cherry stoner if possible). If using canned cherries, drain well, discard the juice and place in the prepared dish.

Sift the flour and salt into a large bowl. Stir in 2 tablespoons of the caster sugar and make a well in the centre. Beat the eggs, then pour into the well of the dry ingredients.

Warm the milk and slowly pour into the well, beating throughout and gradually drawing in the flour from the sides of the bowl. Continue until a smooth batter has formed.

Melt the butter in a small saucepan over a low heat, then stir into the batter with the rum. Reserve for 15 minutes, then beat again until smooth and easy to pour.

Pour into the prepared baking dish and bake in the preheated oven for 30–35 minutes, or until golden brown and set.

Remove the pudding from the oven, sprinkle with the remaining sugar and serve hot with plenty of fresh cream.

Try This: FOR AN ALTERNATIVE: 154 FOR A SAVOURY OPTION: 30

Summer Pavlova

SERVES 6–8

4 medium egg whites
225 g/8 oz caster sugar
1 tsp vanilla essence
2 tsp white wine vinegar
1½ tsp cornflour

300 ml/½ pint half-fat
   Greek-set yogurt
2 tbsp honey
225 g/8 oz strawberries,
   hulled

125 g/4 oz raspberries
125 g/4 oz blueberries
4 kiwis, peeled and sliced
icing sugar, to decorate

Preheat the oven to 150°C/300°F/Gas Mark 2. Line a baking sheet with a sheet of greaseproof or baking parchment paper.

Place the egg whites in a clean grease-free bowl and whisk until very stiff. Whisk in half the sugar, vanilla essence, vinegar and cornflour, continue whisking until stiff. Gradually, whisk in the remaining sugar, a teaspoonful at a time until very stiff and glossy.

Using a large spoon, arrange spoonfuls of the meringue in a circle on the greaseproof paper or baking parchment paper.

Bake in the preheated oven for 1 hour until crisp and dry. Turn the oven off and leave the meringue in the oven to cool completely.

Remove the meringue from the baking sheet and peel away the parchment paper. Mix together the yogurt and honey. Place the pavlova on a serving plate and spoon the yogurt into the centre.

Scatter over the strawberries, raspberries, blueberries and kiwis. Dust with the icing sugar and serve.

Try This: FOR AN ALTERNATIVE: 326 FOR A SAVOURY OPTION: 38

Eve's Pudding

SERVES 6

450 g/1 lb cooking apples	125 g/4 oz caster sugar	125 g/4 oz self-raising flour
175 g/6 oz blackberries	125 g/4 oz butter	1 tbsp icing sugar
75 g/3 oz demerara sugar	few drops of vanilla essence	ready-made custard,
grated rind of 1 lemon	2 medium eggs, beaten	to serve

Preheat the oven to 180°C/350°F/Gas Mark 4. Oil a 1.1 litre/2 pint baking dish.

Peel, core and slice the apples and place a layer in the base of the prepared dish. Sprinkle over some of the blackberries, a little demerara sugar and lemon zest. Continue to layer the apple and blackberries in this way until all the ingredients have been used.

Cream the sugar and butter together until light and fluffy. Beat in the vanilla essence and then the eggs a little at a time, adding a spoonful of flour after each addition. Fold in the extra flour with a metal spoon or rubber spatula and mix well.

Spread the sponge mixture over the top of the fruit and level with the back of a spoon. Place the dish on a baking sheet and bake in the preheated oven for 35–40 minutes, or until well risen and golden brown. (To test if the pudding is cooked, press the cooked sponge lightly with a clean finger – if it springs back the sponge is cooked.)

Dust the pudding with a little icing sugar and serve immediately with the custard.

Try This: FOR AN ALTERNATIVE: 146 FOR A SAVOURY OPTION: 24

Golden Castle Pudding

SERVES 4–6

125 g/4 oz butter
125 g/4 oz caster sugar
a few drops of vanilla

essence
2 medium eggs, beaten
125 g/4 oz self-raising flour

4 tbsp golden syrup
crème fraîche or ready-made
custard, to serve

Preheat the oven to 180°C/350°F/Gas Mark 4. Lightly oil 4–6 individual pudding bowls and place a small circle of lightly oiled non-stick baking or greaseproof paper in the base of each one.

Place the butter and caster sugar in a large bowl, then beat together until the mixture is pale and creamy. Stir in the vanilla essence and gradually add the beaten eggs, a little at a time. Add a tablespoon of flour after each addition of egg and beat well.

When the mixture is smooth, add the remaining flour and fold in gently. Add a tablespoon of water and mix to form a soft mixture that will drop easily off a spoon.

Spoon enough mixture into each basin to come halfway up the tin, allowing enough space for the puddings to rise. Place on a baking sheet and bake in the preheated oven for about 25 minutes until firm and golden brown.

Allow the puddings to stand for 5 minutes. Discard the paper circle and turn out on to individual serving plates.

Warm the golden syrup in a small saucepan and pour a little over each pudding. Serve hot with the crème fraîche or custard.

 Try This: FOR AN ALTERNATIVE: 190   FOR A SAVOURY OPTION: 56

Baked Apple Dumplings

SERVES 4

225 g/8 oz self-raising flour
¼ tsp salt
125 g/4 oz shredded suet

4 medium cooking apples
4–6 tsp luxury mincemeat
1 medium egg white, beaten

2 tsp caster sugar
custard or vanilla sauce,
   to serve

Preheat the oven to 200°C/400°F/Gas Mark 6. Lightly oil a baking tray. Place the flour and salt in a bowl and stir in the suet. Add just enough water to the mixture to mix to a soft but not sticky dough, using the fingertips. Turn the dough on to a lightly floured board and knead lightly into a ball.

Divide the dough into 4 pieces and roll out each piece into a thin square, large enough to encase the apples. Peel and core the apples and place 1 apple in the centre of each square of pastry.

Fill the centre of the apple with mincemeat, brush the edges of each pastry square with water and draw the corners up to meet over each apple.

Press the edges of the pastry firmly together and decorate with pastry leaves and shapes made from the extra pastry trimmings.

Place the apples on the prepared baking tray, brush with the egg white and sprinkle with the sugar. Bake in the preheated oven for 30 minutes or until golden and the pastry and apples are cooked. Serve the dumplings hot with the custard or vanilla sauce.

Try This: FOR AN ALTERNATIVE: 244 FOR A SAVOURY OPTION: 36

Ricotta Cheesecake with Strawberry Coulis

SERVES 6–8

125 g/4 oz digestive biscuits
100 g/3½ oz candied peel, chopped
65 g/2½ oz butter, melted
150 ml/¼ pint crème fraîche

575 g/4 oz ricotta cheese
100 g/3½ oz caster sugar
1 vanilla pod, seeds only
2 large eggs
225 g/8 oz strawberries

25–50 g/1–2 oz caster sugar, to taste
zest and juice of 1 orange

Preheat oven to 170˚C/325˚F/Gas Mark 3. Line a 20.5 cm/8 inch springform tin with baking parchment. Place the biscuits into a food processor together with the peel. Blend until the biscuits are crushed and the peel is chopped. Add 50 g/2 oz of the melted butter and process until mixed. Tip into the tin and spread evenly over the bottom. Press firmly into place and reserve.

Blend together the crème fraîche, ricotta cheese, sugar, vanilla seeds and eggs in a food processor. With the motor running, add the remaining melted butter and blend for a few seconds. Pour the mixture on to the base. Transfer to the preheated oven and cook for about 1 hour, until set and risen round the edges, but slightly wobbly in the centre. Switch off the oven and allow to cool there. chill in the refrigerator for at least 8 hours, or preferably overnight.

Wash and drain the strawberries. Hull the fruit and remove any soft spots. Put into the food processor along with 25 g/1 oz of the sugar and orange juice and zest. Blend until smooth. Add the remaining sugar to taste. Pass through a sieve to remove seeds and chill in the refrigerator until needed.

Cut the cheesecake into wedges, spoon over some of the strawberry coulis and serve.

Try This: FOR AN ALTERNATIVE: 320   FOR A SAVOURY OPTION: 60

Peach & Chocolate Bake

SERVES 6

200 g/7 oz plain dark
   chocolate
125 g/4 oz unsalted butter
4 medium eggs, separated

125 g/4 oz caster sugar
425 g can peach slices,
   drained
½ tsp ground cinnamon

1 tbsp icing sugar, sifted,
   to decorate
crème fraîche, to serve

Preheat the oven to 170°C/325°F/Gas Mark 3, 10 minutes before baking. Lightly oil a 1.7 litre/3 pint ovenproof dish.

Break the chocolate and butter into small pieces and place in a small heatproof bowl set over a saucepan of gently simmering water. Ensure the water is not touching the base of the bowl and leave to melt. Remove the bowl from the heat and stir until smooth.

Whisk the egg yolks with the sugar until very thick and creamy, then stir the melted chocolate and butter into the whisked egg yolk mixture and mix together lightly.

Place the egg whites in a clean grease-free bowl and whisk until stiff, then fold 2 tablespoons of the whisked egg whites into the chocolate mixture. Mix well, then add the remaining egg white and fold in very lightly.

Fold the peach slices and the cinnamon into the mixture, then spoon the mixture into the prepared dish. Do not level the mixture, leave a little uneven.

Bake in the preheated oven for 35–40 minutes, or until well risen and just firm to the touch. Sprinkle the bake with the icing sugar and serve immediately with spoonfuls of crème fraîche.

Try This: FOR AN ALTERNATIVE: 152 FOR A SAVOURY OPTION: 38

Chocolate Pecan Angel Pie

CUTS INTO 8–10 SLICES

4 large egg whites
¼ tsp cream of tartar
225 g/8 oz caster sugar
3 tsp vanilla essence
100 g/3½ oz pecans, lightly

toasted and chopped
75 g/3 oz dark chocolate chips
150 ml/¼ pint double cream
150 g/5 oz white chocolate,
grated

To decorate:
fresh raspberries
dark chocolate curls
few sprigs of fresh mint

Preheat the oven to 110°C/225°F/Gas Mark ¼, 5 minutes before baking. Lightly oil a 23 cm/9 inch pie plate.

Using an electric mixer, whisk the egg whites and cream of tartar on a low speed until foamy, then increase the speed and beat until soft peaks form. Gradually beat in the sugar, 1 tablespoon at a time, beating well after each addition, until stiff glossy peaks form and the sugar is completely dissolved. (Test by rubbing a bit of meringue between your fingers – if gritty, continue beating.) This will take about 15 minutes. Beat in 2 teaspoons of the vanilla essence, then fold in the nuts and the chocolate chips.

Spread the meringue evenly in the pie plate, making a shallow well in the centre and slightly building up the sides. Bake in the preheated oven for 1–1¼ hours or until a golden creamy colour. Lower the oven temperature if the meringue colours too quickly. Turn the oven off, but do not remove the meringue. Leave the oven door ajar (about 5 cm/2 inches) for about 1 hour. Transfer to a wire rack until cold.

Pour the double cream into a small saucepan and bring to the boil. Remove from the heat, add the grated white chocolate and stir until melted. Add the remaining vanilla essence and leave to cool, then whip until thick. Spoon the white chocolate whipped cream into the pie shell, piling it high and swirling decoratively. Decorate with fresh raspberries and chocolate curls. Chill in the refrigerator for 2 hours before serving. When ready to serve, add sprigs of mint on the top and cut into slices.

Try This: FOR AN ALTERNATIVE: 346 FOR A SAVOURY OPTION: 96

Oaty Fruit Puddings

SERVES 4

125 g/4 oz rolled oats
50 g/2 oz low-fat
  spread, melted
2 tbsp chopped almonds
1 tbsp clear honey

pinch of ground cinnamon
2 pears, peeled, cored and
  finely chopped
1 tbsp marmalade
orange zest, to decorate

low-fat custard or fruit-
  flavoured low-fat yogurt,
  to serve

Preheat the oven to 200°C/400°F/Gas Mark 6. Lightly oil and line the bases of 4 individual pudding bowls or muffin tins with a small circle of greaseproof paper.

Mix together the oats, low-fat spread, nuts, honey and cinnamon in a small bowl.

Using a spoon, spread two thirds of the oaty mixture over the base and around the sides of the pudding bowls or muffin tins.

Toss together the pears and marmalade and spoon into the oaty cases. Scatter over the remaining oaty mixture to cover the pears and marmalade. Bake in the preheated oven for 15–20 minutes, until cooked and the tops of the puddings are golden and crisp.

Leave for 5 minutes before removing the pudding bowls or muffin tins. Decorate with orange zest and serve hot with low-fat custard or low-fat fruit-flavoured yogurt.

Try This: FOR AN ALTERNATIVE: 208 FOR A SAVOURY OPTION: 32

Egg Custard Tart

SERVES 6

Sweet pastry:
50 g/2 oz butter
50 g/2 oz white vegetable fat
175 g/6 oz plain flour
1 medium egg yolk, beaten

2 tsp caster sugar

For the filling:
300 ml/½ pint milk
2 medium eggs, plus

1 medium egg yolk
25 g/1 oz caster sugar
½ tsp freshly grated nutmeg

Preheat the oven to 200°C/400°F/Gas Mark 6. Oil a 20.5 cm/8 inch flan tin or dish.

Make the pastry by cutting the butter and vegetable fat into small cubes. Add to the flour in a large bowl and rub in, until the mixture resembles fine breadcrumbs. Add the egg, sugar and enough water to form a soft and pliable dough. Turn on to a lightly floured board and knead. Wrap and chill in the refrigerator for 30 minutes.

Roll the pastry out on to a lightly floured surface or pastry board and use to line the oiled flan tin. Place in the refrigerator to reserve.

Warm the milk in a small saucepan. Briskly whisk together the eggs, egg yolk and caster sugar. Pour the milk into the egg mixture and whisk until blended.

Strain through a sieve into the pastry case. Place the flan tin on a baking sheet. Sprinkle the top of the tart with nutmeg and bake in the preheated oven for about 15 minutes.

Turn the oven down to 170°C/325°F/Gas Mark 3 and bake for a further 30 minutes, or until the custard has set. Serve hot or cold.

Try This: FOR AN ALTERNATIVE: 186 FOR A SAVOURY OPTION: 44

Almond & Pine Nut Tart

SERVES 6

250 g/9 oz ready-made
   sweet shortcrust pastry
75 g/3 oz blanched almonds
75 g/3 oz caster sugar
pinch of salt
2 medium eggs

1 tsp vanilla essence
2–3 drops almond essence
125 g/4 oz unsalted butter,
   softened
2 tbsp flour
½ tsp baking powder

3–4 tbsp raspberry jam
50 g/2 oz pine nuts
icing sugar, to decorate
whipped cream, to serve

Preheat oven to 200°C/400°F/Gas Mark 6. Roll out the pastry and use to line a 23 cm/9 inch fluted flan tin. Chill in the refrigerator for 10 minutes, then line with greaseproof paper and baking beans and bake blind in the preheated oven for 10 minutes. Remove the paper and beans and bake for a further 10–12 minutes until cooked. Leave to cool. Reduce the temperature to 190°C/375°F/Gas Mark 5.

Grind the almonds in a food processor until fine. Add the sugar, salt, eggs, vanilla and almond essence and blend. Add the butter, flour and baking powder and blend until smooth.

Spread a thick layer of the raspberry jam over the cooled pastry case, then pour in the almond filling. Sprinkle the pine nuts evenly over the top and bake for 30 minutes, until firm and browned.

Remove the tart from the oven and leave to cool. Dust generously with icing sugar and serve cut into wedges with whipped cream.

Try This: FOR AN ALTERNATIVE: 214 FOR A SAVOURY OPTION: 26

Raspberry & Almond Tart

SERVES 6–8

For the pastry:
225 g/8 oz plain flour
pinch of salt
125 g/4 oz butter, cut
    into pieces
50 g/2 oz caster sugar
grated zest of ½ lemon

1 medium egg yolk

For the filling:
75 g/3 oz butter
75 g/3 oz caster sugar
75 g/3 oz ground almonds
2 medium eggs

225 g/8 oz raspberries,
    thawed if frozen
2 tbsp slivered or
    flaked almonds
icing sugar for dusting

Preheat oven to 200°C/400°F/Gas Mark 6, 15 minutes before cooking. Blend the flour, salt and butter in a food processor until the mixture resembles breadcrumbs. Add the sugar and lemon zest and blend again for 1 minute. Mix the egg yolk with 2 tablespoons of cold water and add to the mixture. Blend until the mixture starts to come together, adding a little more water if necessary, then tip out on to a lightly floured surface. Knead until smooth, wrap in clingfilm and chill in the refrigerator for 30 minutes.

Roll the dough out thinly on a lightly floured surface and use to line a 23 cm/9 inch fluted tart tin. Chill in the refrigerator for 10 minutes. Line the pastry case with greaseproof paper and baking beans. Bake for 10 minutes, then remove the paper and beans and return to the oven for a further 10–12 minutes until cooked. Allow to cool slightly, then reduce the oven temperature to 190°C/375°F/Gas Mark 5.

Blend together the butter, sugar, ground almonds, and eggs until smooth. Spread the raspberries over the base of the pastry, then cover with the almond mixture. Bake for 15 minutes. Remove from the oven and sprinkle with the slivered or flaked almonds and dust generously with icing sugar. Bake for a further 15–20 minutes, until firm and golden brown. Leave to cool, then serve.

Try This: FOR AN ALTERNATIVE: 204 FOR A SAVOURY OPTION: 86

Strawberry Flan

SERVES 6

Sweet pastry:
175 g/6 oz plain flour
50 g/2 oz butter
50 g/2 oz white vegetable fat
2 tsp caster sugar
1 medium egg yolk, beaten

For the filling:
1 medium egg, plus 1 extra
   egg yolk
50 g/2 oz caster sugar
25 g/1 oz plain flour
300 ml/½ pint milk

few drops of vanilla essence
450 g/1 lb strawberries,
   cleaned and hulled
mint leaves, to decorate

Preheat the oven to 200˚C/400˚F/Gas Mark 6. Place the flour, butter and vegetable fat in a food processor and blend until the mixture resembles fine breadcrumbs. Stir in the sugar, then with the machine running, add the egg yolk and enough water to make a fairly stiff dough. Knead lightly, cover and chill in the refrigerator for 30 minutes.

Roll out the pastry and use to line a 23 cm/9 inch loose-bottomed flan tin. Place a piece of greaseproof paper in the pastry case and cover with baking beans or rice. Bake in the preheated oven for 15–20 minutes, until just firm. Reserve until cool.

Make the filling by whisking the eggs and sugar together until thick and pale. Gradually stir in the flour and then the milk. Pour into a small saucepan and simmer for 3–4 minutes stirring throughout.

Add the vanilla essence to taste, then pour into a bowl and leave to cool. Cover with greaseproof paper to prevent a skin from forming.

When the filling is cold, whisk until smooth then pour on to the cooked flan case. Slice the strawberries and arrange on the top of the filling. Decorate with the mint leaves and serve.

Try This: FOR AN ALTERNATIVE: 320 FOR A SAVOURY OPTION: 68

Goats' Cheese & Lemon Tart

SERVES 8–10

For the pastry:
125 g/4 oz butter, cut into
    small pieces
225 g/8 oz plain flour
pinch of salt
50 g/2 oz caster sugar

1 medium egg yolk

For the filling:
350 g/12 oz mild fresh goats'
    cheese, e.g. Chavroux
3 medium eggs, beaten

150 g/5 oz caster sugar
grated rind and juice of
    3 lemons
450 ml/¾ pint double cream
fresh raspberries, to
    decorate and serve

Preheat oven to 200°C/400°F/Gas Mark 6, 15 minutes before cooking. Rub the butter into the plain flour and salt until the mixture resembles breadcrumbs, then stir in the sugar. Beat the egg yolk with 2 tablespoons of cold water and add to the mixture. Mix together until a dough is formed then turn the dough out on to a lightly floured surface and knead until smooth. Chill in the refrigerator for 30 minutes.

Roll the dough out thinly on a lightly floured surface and use to line a 4 cm/1½ inch deep 23 cm /9 inch fluted flan tin. Chill in the refrigerator for 10 minutes. Line the pastry case with greaseproof paper and baking beans or tinfoil and bake blind in the preheated oven for 10 minutes. Remove the paper and beans or tinfoil. Return to the oven for a further 12–15 minutes until cooked. Leave to cool slightly, then reduce the oven temperature to 150°C/300°F/Gas Mark 2.

Beat the goats' cheese until smooth. Whisk in the eggs, sugar, lemon rind and juice. Add the cream and mix well.

Carefully pour the cheese mixture into the pastry case and return to the oven. Bake in the oven for 35–40 minutes, or until just set. If it begins to brown or swell, open the oven door for 2 minutes, then reduce the temperature to 120°C/250°F/Gas Mark ½ and leave the tart to cool in the oven. Chill in the refrigerator until cold. Decorate and serve with fresh raspberries.

Try This: FOR AN ALTERNATIVE: 332   FOR A SAVOURY OPTION: 76

Rich Double-crust Plum Pie

SERVES 6

For the pastry:
75 g/3 oz butter
75 g/3 oz white vegetable fat
225 g/8 oz plain flour

2 medium egg yolks

For the filling:
450 g/1 lb fresh plums,

preferably Victoria
50 g/2 oz caster sugar
1 tbsp milk
a little extra caster sugar

Preheat the oven to 200°C/400°F/Gas Mark 6. Make the pastry by rubbing the butter and white vegetable fat into the flour until it resembles fine breadcrumbs or blend in a food processor. Add the egg yolks and enough water to make a soft dough. Knead lightly, then wrap and leave in the refrigerator for about 30 minutes.

Meanwhile, prepare the fruit. Rinse and dry the plums, then cut in half and remove the stones. Slice the plums into chunks and cook in a saucepan with 25 g/1 oz of the sugar and 2 tablespoons of water for 5–7 minutes, or until slightly softened. Remove from the heat and add the remaining sugar to taste and allow to cool.

Roll out half the chilled pastry on a lightly floured surface and use to line the base and sides of a 1.1 litre/2 pint pie dish. Allow the pastry to hang over the edge of the dish. Spoon in the prepared plums.

Roll out the remaining pastry to use as the lid and brush the edge with a little water. Wrap the pastry around the rolling pin and place over the plums. Press the edges together to seal and mark a decorative edge around the rim of the pastry by pinching with the thumb and forefinger or using the back of a fork.

Brush the lid with milk, and make a few slits in the top. Use any trimmings to decorate the top of the pie with pastry leaves. Place on a baking sheet and bake in the preheated oven for 30 minutes, or until golden brown. Sprinkle with a little caster sugar and serve hot or cold.

Try This: FOR AN ALTERNATIVE: 184 FOR A SAVOURY OPTION: 70

Fruity Roulade

SERVES 4

For the sponge:
3 medium eggs
75 g/3 oz caster sugar
75 g/3 oz plain flour, sieved
1–2 tbsp caster sugar
    for sprinkling

For the filling:
125 g/4 oz Quark
125 g/4 oz half-fat
    Greek yogurt
25 g/1 oz caster sugar
1 tbsp orange
    liqueur (optional)

grated rind of 1 orange
125 g/4 oz strawberries,
    hulled and cut into quarters

To decorate:
strawberries
sifted icing sugar

Preheat the oven to 220°C/425°F/Gas Mark 7. Lightly oil and line a 33 x 23 cm/13 x 9 inch Swiss roll tin with greaseproof or baking parchment paper.

Using an electric whisk, whisk the eggs and sugar until the mixture is double in volume and leaves a trail across the top. Fold in the flour with a metal spoon or rubber spatula. Pour into the prepared tin and bake in the preheated oven for 10–12 minutes, until well risen and golden.

Place a whole sheet of greaseproof or baking parchment paper out on a flat work surface and sprinkle evenly with caster sugar.

Turn the cooked sponge out on to the paper, trim the sponge and roll up encasing the paper inside. Reserve until cool.

To make the filling, mix together the Quark, yogurt, caster sugar, liqueur (if using) and orange rind. Unroll the roulade, discard the paper and spread over the mixture. Scatter over the strawberries and roll up.

Decorate the roulade with the strawberries. Dust with the icing sugar and serve.

Try This: FOR AN ALTERNATIVE: 330 FOR A SAVOURY OPTION: 78

Mocha Pie

SERVES 4–6

1 x 23 cm/9 inch ready-made
   sweet pastry case

For the filling:
125 g/4 oz plain dark
   chocolate, broken
   into pieces

175g/6 oz unsalted butter
225 g/8 oz soft brown sugar
1 tsp vanilla essence
3 tbsp strong black coffee

For the topping:
600 ml/1 pint double cream

50 g/2 oz icing sugar
2 tsp vanilla essence
1 tsp instant coffee
   dissolved in 1 tsp boiling
   water and cooled
grated plain and white
   chocolate, to decorate

Place the prepared pastry case on a large serving plate and reserve. Melt the chocolate in a heatproof bowl set over a saucepan of simmering water. Ensure the water is not touching the base of the bowl. Remove from the heat, stir until smooth and leave to cool.

Cream the butter, soft brown sugar and vanilla essence until light and fluffy, then beat in the cooled chocolate. Add the strong black coffee, pour into the pastry case and chill in the refrigerator for about 30 minutes.

For the topping, whisk the cream until beginning to thicken, then whisk in the sugar and vanilla essence. Continue to whisk until the cream is softly peaking. Spoon just under half of the cream into a separate bowl and fold in the dissolved coffee.

Spread the remaining cream over the filling in the pastry case. Spoon the coffee-flavoured whipped cream evenly over the top, then swirl it decoratively with a palate knife. Sprinkle with grated chocolate and chill in the refrigerator until ready to serve.

Try This: FOR AN ALTERNATIVE: 338 FOR A SAVOURY OPTION: 64

Iced Bakewell Tart

CUTS INTO 8 SLICES

For the rich pastry:
175 g/6 oz plain flour
pinch of salt
60 g/2½ oz butter, cut into
  small pieces
50 g/2 oz white vegetable
  fat, cut into small pieces
2 small egg yolks, beaten

For the filling:
125 g/4 oz butter, melted
125 g/4 oz caster sugar
125 g/4 oz ground almonds
2 large eggs, beaten
few drops of almond
  essence
2 tbsp seedless raspberry jam

For the icing:
125 g/4 oz icing sugar, sifted
6–8 tsp fresh lemon juice
25 g/1 oz toasted flaked
  almonds

Preheat the oven to 200°C/400°F/Gas Mark 6. Place the flour and salt in a bowl, rub in the butter and vegetable fat until the mixture resembles breadcrumbs. Alternatively, blend quickly, in short bursts in a food processor.

Add the eggs with sufficient water to make a soft, pliable dough. Knead lightly on a floured board then chill in the refrigerator for about 30 minutes. Roll out the pastry and use to line a 23 cm/9 inch loose-bottomed flan tin.

For the filling, mix together the melted butter, sugar, almonds and beaten eggs and add a few drops of almond essence. Spread the base of the pastry case with the raspberry jam and spoon over the egg mixture. Bake in the preheated oven for about 30 minutes, or until the filling is firm and golden brown. Remove from the oven and allow to cool completely.

When the tart is cold make the icing by mixing together the icing sugar and lemon juice, a little at a time, until the icing is smooth and of a spreadable consistency. Spread the icing over the tart, leave to set for 2–3 minutes and sprinkle with the almonds. Chill in the refrigerator for about 10 minutes and serve.

Try This: FOR AN ALTERNATIVE: 172 FOR A SAVOURY OPTION: 28

White Chocolate Mousse & Strawberry Tart

CUTS INTO 10 SLICES

1 quantity ready-made sweet shortcrust pastry
60 g/2½ oz strawberry jam
1–2 tbsp kirsch or framboise liqueur
450–700 g/1–1½ lb ripe

strawberries, sliced lengthways

For the white chocolate mousse:
250 g/9 oz white chocolate,

chopped
350 ml/12 oz double cream
3 tbsp kirsch or framboise liqueur
1–2 large egg whites (optional)

Preheat the oven to 200°C/400°F/Gas Mark 6, 15 minutes before baking. Roll the pastry out on a lightly floured surface and use to line a 25.5 cm/10 inch flan tin. Line with either tinfoil or nonstick baking parchment and baking beans then bake blind in the preheated oven for 15–20 minutes. Remove the tinfoil or baking parchment and return to the oven for 5 more minutes.

To make the mousse, place the white chocolate with 2 tablespoons of water and 125 ml/4 fl oz of the cream in a saucepan and heat gently, stirring until the chocolate has melted and is smooth. Remove from the heat, stir in the kirsch or framboise liqueur and cool.

Whip the remaining cream until soft peaks form. Fold a spoonful of the cream into the cooled white chocolate mixture, then fold in the remaining cream. If using, whisk the egg whites until stiff and gently fold into the white chocolate cream mixture to make a softer, lighter mousse. Chill in the refrigerator for 15–20 minutes. Heat the strawberry jam with the kirsch or framboise liqueur and brush or spread half the mixture onto the pastry base. Leave to cool.

Spread the chilled chocolate mousse over the jam and arrange the sliced strawberries in concentric circles over the mousse. If necessary, reheat the strawberry jam and glaze the strawberries lightly. Chill the tart in the refrigerator for about 3–4 hours, or until the chocolate mousse has set. Cut into slices and serve.

Try This: FOR AN ALTERNATIVE: 176 FOR A SAVOURY OPTION: 54

Lattice Treacle Tart

SERVES 4

For the pastry:
175 g/6 oz plain flour
40 g/1½ oz butter
40 g/1½ oz white vegetable fat

For the filling:
225 g/8 oz golden syrup
finely grated rind and juice
   of 1 lemon

75 g/3 oz fresh white
   breadcrumbs
1 small egg, beaten

Preheat the oven to 190°C/375°F/Gas Mark 5. Make the pastry by placing the flour, butter and white vegetable fat in a food processor. Blend in short sharp bursts until the mixture resembles fine breadcrumbs. Remove from the processor and place on a pastry board or in a large bowl.

Stir in enough cold water to make a dough and knead in a large bowl or on a floured surface until smooth and pliable.

Roll out the pastry and use to line a 20.5 cm/8 inch loose-bottomed fluted flan dish or tin. Reserve the pastry trimmings for decoration. Chill for 30 minutes.

Meanwhile, to make the filling, place the golden syrup in a saucepan and warm gently with the lemon rind and juice. Tip the breadcrumbs into the pastry case and pour the syrup mixture over the top.

Roll the pastry trimmings out on a lightly floured surface and cut into 6–8 thin strips. Lightly dampen the pastry edge of the tart, then place the strips across the filling in a lattice pattern. Brush the ends of the strips with water and seal to the edge of the tart. Brush a little beaten egg over the pastry and bake in the preheated oven for a 25 minutes, or until the filling is just set. Serve hot or cold.

Raspberry Chocolate Ganache & Berry Tartlets

SERVES 8

1 quantity chocolate pastry (*see* page 194)	raspberry jam	other summer berries
600 ml/1 pint whipping cream	225 g/8 oz plain dark chocolate, chopped	50 ml/2 fl oz framboise liqueur
275 g/10 oz seedless	700 g/1½ lb raspberries or	1 tbsp caster sugar
		crème fraîche, to serve

Preheat the oven to 200°C/400°F/Gas Mark 6, 15 minutes before cooking. Make the chocolate pastry and use to line 8 x 7.5 cm/3 inch tartlet tins. Bake blind in the preheated oven for 12 minutes.

Place 400 ml/14 fl oz of the cream and half of the raspberry jam in a saucepan and bring to the boil, whisking constantly to dissolve the jam. Remove from the heat and add the chocolate all at once, stirring until the chocolate has melted.

Pour into the pastry-lined tartlet tins, shaking gently to distribute the ganache evenly. Chill in the refrigerator for 1 hour or until set.

Place the berries in a large shallow bowl. Heat the remaining raspberry jam with half the framboise liqueur over a medium heat until melted and bubbling. Drizzle over the berries and toss gently to coat.

Divide the berries among the tartlets, piling them up if necessary. Chill in the refrigerator until ready to serve.

Remove the tartlets from the refrigerator for at least 30 minutes before serving. Using an electric whisk, whisk the remaining cream with the caster sugar and the remaining framboise liqueur until it is thick and softly peaking. Serve with the tartlets and crème fraîche.

Try This: FOR AN ALTERNATIVE: 322 FOR A SAVOURY OPTION: 72

Pear & Chocolate Custard Tart

SERVES 6

For the chocolate pastry:
125 g/4 oz unsalted butter, softened
60 g/2½ oz caster sugar
2 tsp vanilla essence
175 g/6 oz plain flour, sifted

40 g/1½ oz cocoa powder
whipped cream, to serve

For the filling:
125 g/4 oz plain dark chocolate, chopped

225 ml/8 fl oz whipping cream
50 g/2 oz caster sugar
1 large egg
1 large egg yolk
1 tbsp crème de cacao
3 ripe pears

Preheat the oven to 190°C/375°F/Gas Mark 5, 10 minutes before baking. To make the pastry, put the butter, sugar and vanilla essence into a food processor and blend until creamy. Add the flour and cocoa powder and process until a soft dough forms. Remove the dough, wrap in clingfilm and chill in the refrigerator for at least 1 hour. Roll out the dough between 2 sheets of clingfilm to a 28 cm/11 inch round. Peel off the top sheet of clingfilm and invert the pastry round into a lightly oiled 23 cm/9 inch loose-based flan tin, easing the dough into the base and sides. Prick the base with a fork, then chill in the refrigerator for 1 hour. Place a sheet of nonstick baking parchment and baking beans in the case and bake blind in the preheated oven for 10 minutes. Remove the parchment and beans and bake for a further 5 minutes. Remove and cool.

To make the filling, heat the chocolate, cream and half the sugar in a medium saucepan over a low heat, stirring until melted and smooth. Remove from the heat and cool slightly before beating in the egg, egg yolk and crème de cacao. Spread evenly over the pastry case base. Peel the pears, then cut each pear in half and carefully remove the core. Cut each half crossways into thin slices and arrange over the custard, gently fanning the slices towards the centre and pressing into the chocolate custard. Bake in the oven for 10 minutes. Reduce the oven temperature to 180°C/350°F/Gas Mark 4 and sprinkle the surface evenly with the remaining sugar. Bake in the oven for 20–25 minutes, or until the custard is set and the pears are tender and glazed. Remove from the oven and leave to cool slightly. Cut into slices, then serve with spoonfuls of whipped cream.

Try This: FOR AN ALTERNATIVE: 174 FOR A SAVOURY OPTION: 40

Double Chocolate Truffle Slice

CUTS INTO 12–14 SLICES

1 quantity Chocolate Pastry
  (*see* page 194)
300 ml/½ pint double cream
300 g/11 oz plain dark

chocolate, chopped
25–40 g/1–1½ oz unsalted
  butter, diced
50 ml/2 fl oz brandy or liqueur

icing sugar or cocoa powder
  for dusting

Preheat the oven to 200°C/400°F/Gas Mark 6, 15 minutes before baking. Prepare the chocolate pastry and chill in the refrigerator, according to instructions.

Roll the dough out to a rectangle about 38 x 15 cm/15 x 6 inches and use to line a rectangular loose-based flan tin, trim then chill in the refrigerator for 1 hour.

Place a sheet of nonstick baking parchment and baking beans in the pastry case, then bake blind in the preheated oven for 20 minutes. Remove the baking parchment and beans and bake for 10 minutes more. Leave to cool completely.

Bring the cream to the boil. Remove from the heat and add the chocolate all at once, stirring until melted and smooth. Beat in the butter, then stir in the brandy liqueur. Leave to cool slightly, then pour into the cooked pastry shell. Refrigerate until set.

Cut out 2.5 cm/1 inch strips of nonstick baking parchment. Place over the tart in a crisscross pattern and dust with icing sugar or cocoa.

Arrange chocolate leaves, caraque or curls around the edges of the tart. Refrigerate until ready to serve. Leave to soften at room temperature for 15 minutes before serving.

Try This: FOR AN ALTERNATIVE: 296   FOR A SAVOURY OPTION: 76

Chocolate Roulade

SERVES 8

150 g/5 oz golden caster sugar
5 medium eggs, separated
50 g/2 oz cocoa powder

For the filling:
300 ml/½ pint double cream
3 tbsp whisky
50 g/2 oz creamed coconut,

chilled
2 tbsp icing sugar
coarsely shredded coconut,
toasted

Preheat the oven to 180°C/350°F/Gas Mark 4, 10 minutes before baking. Oil and line a 33 x 23 cm /13 x 9 inch Swiss roll tin with a single sheet of nonstick baking parchment. Dust a large sheet of baking parchment with 2 tablespoons of the caster sugar.

Place the egg yolks in a bowl with the remaining sugar, set over a saucepan of gently simmering water and whisk until pale and thick. Sift the cocoa powder into the mixture and carefully fold in.

Whisk the egg whites in a clean, grease-free bowl until soft peaks form. Gently add 1 tablespoon of the whisked egg whites into the chocolate mixture then fold in the remaining whites. Spoon the mixture onto the prepared tin, smoothing the mixture into the corners. Bake in the preheated oven for 20–25 minutes, or until risen and springy to the touch.

Turn the cooked roulade out onto the sugar-dusted baking parchment and carefully peel off the lining paper. Cover with a clean damp tea towel and leave to cool.

To make the filling, pour the cream and whisky into a bowl and whisk until the cream holds its shape. Grate in the chilled creamed coconut, add the icing sugar and gently stir in. Uncover the roulade and spoon about three-quarters of coconut cream on the roulade and roll up. Spoon the remaining cream on the top and sprinkle with the coconut, then serve.

Try This: FOR AN ALTERNATIVE: 238 FOR A SAVOURY OPTION: 92

Jam Roly Poly

SERVES 6

225 g/8 oz self-raising flour	about 150 ml/¼ pint water	1 tsp caster sugar
¼ tsp salt	3 tbsp strawberry jam	ready-made jam sauce,
125 g/4 oz shredded suet	1 tbsp milk, to glaze	to serve

Preheat the oven to 200°C/400°F/Gas Mark 6. Make the pastry by sifting the flour and salt into a large bowl. Add the suet and mix lightly, then add the water a little at a time and mix to form a soft and pliable dough. (Take care not to make the dough too wet.) Turn the dough out on to a lightly floured board and knead gently until smooth. Roll the dough out into a 23 cm/9 inch x 28 cm/11 inch rectangle.

Spread the jam over the pastry leaving a border of 1 cm/½ inch all round. Fold the border over the jam and brush the edges with water.

Lightly roll the rectangle up from one of the short sides, seal the top edge and press the ends together. (Do not roll the pudding up too tightly.) Turn the pudding upside down on to a large piece of greaseproof paper large enough to come halfway up the sides. (If using non-stick paper, then oil lightly.)

Tie the ends of the paper, to make a boat-shaped paper case for the pudding to sit in and to leave plenty of room for the roly poly to expand. Brush the pudding lightly with milk and sprinkle with the sugar. Bake in the preheated oven for 30–40 minutes, or until well risen and golden. Serve immediately with the jam sauce.

Mini Pistachio & Chocolate Strudels

MAKES 24

5 large sheets filo pastry
50 g/2 oz butter, melted
1–2 tbsp caster sugar
   for sprinkling
50 g/2 oz white chocolate,
   melted, to decorate

For the filling:
125 g/4 oz unsalted
   pistachios, finely chopped
3 tbsp caster sugar
50 g/2 oz plain dark
   chocolate, finely chopped

1–2 tsp rosewater
1 tbsp icing sugar for dusting

Preheat the oven to 170˚C/325˚F/Gas Mark 3, 10 minutes before baking. Lightly oil 2 large baking sheets. For the filling, mix the finely chopped pistachio nuts, the sugar and dark chocolate in a bowl. Sprinkle with the rosewater and stir lightly together and reserve.

Cut each filo pastry sheet into 4 to make 23 x 18 cm/9 x 7 inch rectangles. Place 1 rectangle on the work surface and brush with a little melted butter. Place another rectangle on top and brush with a little more butter. Sprinkle with a little caster sugar and spread about 1 dessertspoon of the filling along one short end. Fold the short end over the filling, then fold in the long edges and roll up. Place on the baking sheet seam-side down. Continue with the remaining pastry sheets and filling until both are used.

Brush each strudel with the remaining melted butter and sprinkle with a little caster sugar. Bake in the preheated oven for 20 minutes, or until golden brown and the pastry is crisp.

Remove from the oven and leave on the baking sheet for 2 minutes, then transfer to a wire rack. Dust with icing sugar. Place the melted white chocolate in a small piping bag fitted with a plain writing pipe and pipe squiggles over the strudel. Leave to set before serving.

Try This: FOR AN ALTERNATIVE: 204   FOR A SAVOURY OPTION: 66

Chocolate Raspberry Mille Feuille

SERVES 6

450 g/1 lb puff pastry,
  thawed if frozen
1 quantity chocolate
  raspberry ganache
  (*see* page 192), chilled
700 g/1½ lbs fresh

raspberries, plus extra
  for decorating
icing sugar for dusting

For the raspberry sauce:
225 g/8 oz fresh raspberries

2 tbsp seedless raspberry jam
1–2 tbsp caster sugar, or
  to taste
2 tbsp lemon juice or
  framboise liqueur

Preheat the oven to 200°C/400°F/Gas Mark 6, 15 minutes before baking. Lightly oil a large baking sheet and sprinkle with a little water. Roll out the pastry on a lightly floured surface to a rectangle about 43 x 28 cm/17 x 11 inches. Cut into 3 long strips. Mark each strip crossways at 6.5 cm/2½ inch intervals using a sharp knife; this will make cutting the baked pastry easier and neater. Carefully transfer to the baking sheet, keeping the edges as straight as possible. Bake in the preheated oven for 20 minutes or until well risen and golden brown. Place on a wire rack and leave to cool. Carefully transfer each rectangle to a work surface and using a sharp knife, trim the long edges straight. Cut along the knife marks to make 18 rectangles.

Place all the ingredients for the raspberry sauce in a food processor and blend until smooth. If the purée is too thick, add a little water. Taste and adjust the sweetness if necessary. Strain into a bowl, cover and chill in the refrigerator.

Place 1 pastry rectangle on the work surface flat- side down, spread with a little chocolate ganache and sprinkle with a few fresh raspberries. Spread a second rectangle with a little ganache, place over the first, pressing gently, then sprinkle with a few raspberries. Place a third rectangle on top, flat-side up, and spread with a little chocolate ganache. Arrange some raspberries on top and dust lightly with a little icing sugar. Repeat with the remaining pastry rectangles, chocolate ganache and fresh raspberries. Chill in the refrigerator until required and serve with the raspberry sauce and any remaining fresh raspberries.

Try This: FOR AN ALTERNATIVE: 192   FOR A SAVOURY OPTION: 50

Biscuits, Cookies, Brownies & Traybakes

Fruit & Nut Flapjacks

MAKES 12

75 g/3 oz butter or margarine
125 g/4 oz soft light
   brown sugar
3 tbsp golden syrup

50 g/2 oz raisins
50 g/2 oz walnuts,
   roughly chopped
175 g/6 oz rolled oats

50 g/2 oz icing sugar
1–1½ tbsp lemon juice

Preheat the oven to 180°C/350°F/Gas Mark 4, 10 minutes before baking. Lightly oil a 23 cm/ 9 inch square cake tin.

Melt the butter or margarine with the sugar and syrup in a small saucepan over a low heat. Remove from the heat.

Stir the raisins, walnuts and oats into the syrup mixture and mix together well. Spoon evenly into the prepared tin and press down well. Transfer to the preheated oven and bake for 20–25 minutes. Remove from the oven and leave to cool in the tin. Cut into bars while still warm.

Sift the icing sugar into a small bowl then gradually beat in the lemon juice a little at a time to form a thin icing. Place into an icing bag fitted with a writing nozzle then pipe thin lines over the flapjacks. Allow to cool and serve.

Try This: FOR AN ALTERNATIVE: 154   FOR A SAVOURY OPTION: 30

Italian Biscotti

MAKES 26–28 BISCUITS

150 g/5 oz butter
200 g/7 oz caster sugar
¼ tsp vanilla essence

1 small egg, beaten
¼ tsp ground cinnamon
grated rind of 1 lemon

15 g/ ½ oz ground almonds
150 g/5 oz plain flour
150 g/5 oz plain dark chocolate

Preheat the oven to 190°C/375°F/Gas Mark 5, 10 minutes before baking. Lightly oil 3–4 baking sheets and reserve. Cream the butter and sugar together in a bowl and mix in the vanilla essence. When it is light and fluffy beat in the egg with the cinnamon, lemon rind and the ground almonds. Stir in the flour to make a firm dough.

Knead lightly until smooth and free from cracks. Shape the dough into rectangular blocks about 4 cm/1½ inches in diameter, wrap in greaseproof paper and chill in the refrigerator for at least 2 hours.

Cut the chilled dough into 5 mm/¼ inch slices, place on the baking sheets and cook in the preheated oven for 12–15 minutes or until firm. Remove from the oven, cool slightly, then transfer to wire racks to cool.

When completely cold, melt the chocolate in a heatproof bowl set over a saucepan of simmering water. Alternatively, melt the chocolate in the microwave according to the manufacturer's instructions. Spoon into a piping bag and pipe over the biscuits. Leave to dry on a sheet of nonstick baking parchment before serving.

Try This: FOR AN ALTERNATIVE: 218   FOR A SAVOURY OPTION: 74

Cantuccini

MAKES 24 BISCUITS

250 g/9 oz plain flour
250 g/9 oz caster sugar
½ tsp baking powder
½ tsp vanilla essence
2 medium eggs

1 medium egg yolk
100 g/3½ oz mixed almonds
    and hazelnuts, toasted
    and roughly chopped
1 tsp whole aniseed

1 medium egg yolk mixed
    with 1 tbsp water, to glaze
Vin Santo or coffee, to serve

Preheat oven to 180°C/350°F/Gas Mark 4. Line a large baking sheet with non-stick baking parchment. Place the flour, caster sugar, baking powder, vanilla essence, the whole eggs and one of the egg yolks into a food processor and blend until the mixture forms a ball, scraping down the sides once or twice. Turn the mixture out on to a lightly floured surface and knead in the chopped nuts and aniseed.

Divide the paste into 3 pieces and roll into logs about 4 cm/1½ inches wide. Place the logs on to the baking sheet at least 5 cm/2 inches apart. Brush lightly with the other egg yolk beaten with 1 tablespoon of water and bake in the preheated oven for 30–35 minutes.

Remove from the oven and reduce the oven temperature to 150°C/300°F/Gas Mark 2. Cut the logs diagonally into 2.5 cm/ 1 inch slices and lay cut-side down on the baking sheet. Return to the oven for a further 30–40 minutes, or until dry and firm. Cool on a wire rack and store in an airtight container. Serve with Vin Santo or coffee.

Try This: FOR AN ALTERNATIVE: 214   FOR A SAVOURY OPTION: 24

Almond & Pistachio Biscotti

MAKES 12 BISCUITS

125 g/4 oz ground almonds
50 g/2 oz shelled pistachios
50 g/2 oz blanched almonds
2 medium eggs

1 medium egg yolk
125 g/4 oz icing sugar
225 g/8 oz plain flour
1 tsp baking powder

pinch of salt
zest of ½ lemon

Preheat oven to 180°C/350°F/Gas Mark 4. Line a large baking sheet with non-stick baking parchment. Toast the ground almonds and whole nuts lightly and reserve until cool.

Beat together the eggs, egg yolk and icing sugar until thick, then beat in the flour, baking powder and salt. Add the lemon zest, ground almonds and whole nuts and mix to form a slightly sticky dough.

Turn the dough on to a lightly floured surface and, using lightly floured hands, form into a log measuring approximately 30 cm/12 inches long. Place down the centre of the prepared baking sheet and transfer to the preheated oven. Bake for 20 minutes.

Remove from the oven and increase the oven temperature to 200°C/400°F/Gas Mark 6. Cut the log diagonally into 2.5 cm/1 inch slices. Return to the baking sheet, cut-side down and bake for a further 10–15 minutes until golden, turning once after 10 minutes. Leave to cool on a wire rack and store in an airtight container.

Try This: FOR AN ALTERNATIVE: 172 FOR A SAVOURY OPTION: 50

Coconut & Almond Munchies

SERVES 26–30

5 medium egg whites
250 g/9 oz icing sugar,
   plus extra to sprinkle

225 g/8 oz ground almonds
200 g/7 oz desiccated
   coconut

grated rind of 1 lemon
125 g/4 oz milk chocolate
125 g/4 oz white chocolate

Preheat the oven to 150°C/300°F/Gas Mark 2, 10 minutes before baking. Line several baking sheets with rice paper. Place the egg whites in a clean, grease-free bowl and whisk until stiff and standing in peaks. Sift the icing sugar, then carefully fold half of the sugar into the whisked egg whites together with the ground almonds. Add the coconut, the remaining icing sugar and the lemon rind and mix together to form a very sticky dough.

Place the mixture in a piping bag and pipe the mixture into walnut-sized mounds onto the rice paper, then sprinkle with a little extra icing sugar. Bake in the preheated oven for 20–25 minutes, or until set and golden on the outside. Remove from the oven and leave to cool slightly. Using a spatula, carefully transfer to a wire rack and leave until cold.

Break the milk and white chocolate into pieces and place in 2 separate bowls. Melt both chocolates set over saucepans of gently simmering water. Alternatively, melt in the microwave, according to the manufacturer's instructions. Stir until smooth and free from lumps. Dip one edge of each munchie in the milk chocolate and leave to dry on nonstick baking parchment. When dry, dip the other side into the white chocolate. Leave to set, then serve as soon as possible.

Try This: FOR AN ALTERNATIVE: 324   FOR A SAVOURY OPTION: 92

Chequered Biscuits

MAKES 20

150 g/5 oz butter
75 g/3 oz icing sugar

pinch of salt
200 g/7 oz plain flour

25 g/1 oz cocoa powder
1 small egg white

Preheat the oven to 190°C/375°F/Gas Mark 5, 10 minutes before baking. Lightly oil 3–4 baking sheets. Place the butter and icing sugar in a bowl and cream together until light and fluffy.

Add the salt, then gradually add the flour, beating well after each addition. Mix well to form a firm dough. Cut the dough in half and knead the cocoa powder into one half. Wrap both portions of dough separately in clingfilm and then leave to chill in the refrigerator for 2 hours.

Divide each piece of dough into 3 portions. Roll each portion of dough into a long roll and arrange these rolls on top of each other to form a chequerboard design, sealing them with egg white. Wrap in clingfilm and refrigerate for 1 hour.

Cut the dough into 5 mm/¼ inch thick slices, place on the baking sheets and bake in the preheated oven for 10–15 minutes. Remove from the oven, and leave to cool for a few minutes. Transfer to a wire rack and leave until cold before serving. Store in an airtight tin.

Try This: FOR AN ALTERNATIVE: 210   FOR A SAVOURY OPTION: 64

Chocolate Chip Cookies

MAKES 36 BISCUITS

175 g/6 oz plain flour
pinch of salt
1 tsp baking powder

¼ tsp bicarbonate of soda
75 g/3 oz butter or margarine
50 g/2 oz soft light

brown sugar
3 tbsp golden syrup
125 g/4 oz chocolate chips

Preheat the oven to 190˚C/375˚F/Gas Mark 5, 10 minutes before baking. Lightly oil a large baking sheet.

In a large bowl, sift together the flour, salt, baking powder and bicarbonate of soda. Cut the butter or margarine into small pieces and add to the flour mixture.

Using 2 knives or the fingertips, rub in the butter or margarine until the mixture resembles coarse breadcrumbs. Add the light brown sugar, golden syrup and chocolate chips. Mix together until a smooth dough forms.

Shape the mixture into small balls and arrange on the baking sheet, leaving enough space to allow them to expand. (These cookies do not increase in size by a great deal, but allow a little space for expansion.)

Flatten the mixture slightly with the fingertips or the heel of the hand. Bake in the preheated oven for 12–15 minutes, or until golden and cooked through.

Allow to cool slightly, then transfer the biscuits on to a wire rack to cool. Serve when cold or otherwise store in an airtight tin.

Try This: FOR AN ALTERNATIVE: 252   FOR A SAVOURY OPTION: 94

Chocolate & Hazelnut Cookies

MAKES 12

75 g/3 oz blanched hazelnuts
100 g/3½ oz caster sugar
50 g/2 oz unsalted butter
pinch of salt

5 tsp cocoa powder
3 tbsp double cream
2 large egg whites
40 g/1½ oz plain flour

2 tbsp rum
75 g/3 oz white chocolate

Preheat the oven to 180°C/350°F/Gas Mark 4, 10 minutes before baking. Lightly oil and flour 2–3 baking sheets. Chop 25 g/1 oz of the hazelnuts and reserve. Blend the remaining hazelnuts with the caster sugar in a food processor until finely ground. Add the butter to the processor bowl and blend until pale and creamy.

Add the salt, cocoa powder and the double cream and mix well. Scrape the mixture into a bowl, using a spatula, and stir in the egg whites. Sift the flour, then stir into the mixture together with the rum.

Spoon heaped tablespoons of the batter onto the baking sheets and sprinkle over a few of the reserved hazelnuts. Bake in the preheated oven for 5–7 minutes or until firm. Remove the cookies from the oven and leave to cool for 1–2 minutes. Using a spatula, transfer to wire racks and leave to cool.

When the biscuits are cold, melt the chocolate in a heatproof bowl set over a saucepan of simmering water. Stir until smooth, then drizzle a little of the chocolate over the top of each biscuit. Leave to dry on a wire rack before serving.

Try This: FOR AN ALTERNATIVE: 340   FOR A SAVOURY OPTION: 26

Almond Macaroons

MAKES 12

rice paper
125 g/4 oz caster sugar
50 g/2 oz ground almonds

1 tsp ground rice
2–3 drops almond essence
1 medium egg white

8 blanched almonds, halved

Preheat the oven to 150°C/300°F/Gas Mark 2, 10 minutes before baking. Line a baking sheet with the rice paper.

Mix the caster sugar, ground almonds, ground rice and almond essence together and reserve.

Whisk the egg white until stiff then gently fold in the caster sugar mixture with a metal spoon or rubber spatula. Mix to form a stiff but not sticky paste. (If the mixture is very sticky, add a little extra ground almonds.)

Place small spoonfuls of the mixture, about the size of an apricot, well apart on the rice paper.

Place a half-blanched almond in the centre of each. Place in the preheated oven and bake for 25 minutes, or until just pale golden.

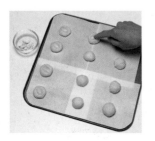

Remove the biscuits from the oven and leave to cool for a few minutes on the baking sheet. Cut or tear the rice paper around the macaroons to release them. Once cold, serve or otherwise store them in an airtight tin.

 Try This: FOR AN ALTERNATIVE: 308   FOR A SAVOURY OPTION: 42

Lemon–iced Ginger Squares

MAKES 12

225 g/8 oz caster sugar
50 g/2 oz butter, melted
2 tbsp black treacle
2 medium egg whites,
    lightly whisked

225 g/8 oz plain flour
1 tsp bicarbonate of soda
½ tsp ground cloves
1 tsp ground cinnamon
¼ tsp ground ginger

pinch of salt
225 ml/8 fl oz buttermilk
175 g/6 oz icing sugar
lemon juice

Preheat the oven to 200°C/400°F/Gas Mark 6, 15 minutes before baking. Lightly oil a 20.5 cm /8 inch square cake tin and sprinkle with a little flour.

Mix together the caster sugar, butter and treacle. Stir in the egg whites. Mix together the flour, bicarbonate of soda, cloves, cinnamon, ginger and salt. Stir the flour mixture and buttermilk alternately into the butter mixture until blended well.

Spoon into the prepared tin and bake in the preheated oven for 35 minutes, or until a skewer inserted into the centre of the cake comes out clean.

Remove from the oven and allow to cool for 5 minutes in the tin before turning out on to a wire rack over a large plate. Using a cocktail stick make holes on the top of the cake.

Meanwhile, mix together the icing sugar with enough lemon juice to make a smooth pourable icing. Carefully pour the icing over the hot cake, then leave until cold. Cut the ginger cake into squares and serve.

Try This: FOR AN ALTERNATIVE: 148 FOR A SAVOURY OPTION: 28

Chocolate Fudge Brownies

MAKES 16

125 g/4 oz butter
175 g/6 oz plain dark
    chocolate, roughly
    chopped or broken

225 g/8 oz caster sugar
2 tsp vanilla essence
2 medium eggs,
    lightly beaten

150 g/5 oz plain flour
175 g/6 oz icing sugar
2 tbsp cocoa powder
15 g/½ oz butter

Preheat the oven to 180°C/350°F/Gas Mark 4, 10 minutes before baking. Lightly oil and line a 20.5 cm/8 inch square cake tin with greaseproof or baking paper.

Slowly melt the butter and chocolate together in a heatproof bowl set over a sauce-pan of simmering water. Transfer the mixture to a large bowl.

Stir in the sugar and vanilla essence, then stir in the eggs. Sift over the flour and fold together well with a metal spoon or rubber spatula. Pour into the prepared tin.

Transfer to the preheated oven and bake for 30 minutes until just set. Remove the cooked mixture from the oven and leave to cool in the tin before turning it out on to a wire rack.

Sift the icing sugar and cocoa powder into a small bowl and make a well in the centre. Place the butter in the well then gradually add about 2 tablespoons of hot water. Mix to form a smooth spreadable icing.

Pour the icing over the cooked mixture. Allow the icing to set before cutting into squares. Serve the brownies when they are cold.

Try This: FOR AN ALTERNATIVE: 286   FOR A SAVOURY OPTION: 76

Triple Chocolate Brownies

MAKES 15

350 g/12 oz plain dark
  chocolate, broken
  into pieces
225 g/8 oz butter, cubed
225 g/8 oz caster sugar

3 large eggs, lightly beaten
1 tsp vanilla essence
2 tbsp very strong black coffee
100 g/3½ oz self-raising flour
125 g/4 oz pecans,

roughly chopped
75 g/3 oz white chocolate,
  roughly chopped
75 g/3 oz milk chocolate,
  roughly chopped

Preheat the oven to 190°C/375°F/Gas Mark 5, 10 minutes before baking. Oil and line a 28 x 18 x 2.5 cm/11 x 7 x 1 inch cake tin with nonstick baking parchment.

Place the plain chocolate in a heatproof bowl with the butter set over a saucepan of almost boiling water and stir occasionally until melted. Remove from the heat and leave until just cool, but not beginning to set.

Place the caster sugar, eggs, vanilla essence and coffee in a large bowl and beat together until smooth. Gradually beat in the chocolate mixture.

Sift the flour into the chocolate mixture. Add the pecans and the white and milk chocolate and gently fold in until mixed thoroughly.

Spoon the mixture into the prepared tin and level the top. Bake on the centre shelf of the preheated oven for 45 minutes, or until just firm to the touch in the centre and crusty on top. Leave to cool in the tin, then turn out onto a wire rack. Trim off the crusty edges and cut into 15 squares. Store in an airtight container.

Try This: FOR AN ALTERNATIVE: 282   FOR A SAVOURY OPTION: 42

Marbled Toffee Shortbread

MAKES 12

175 g/6 oz butter
75 g/3 oz caster sugar
175 g/6 oz plain flour
25 g/1 oz cocoa powder
75 g/3 oz fine semolina

For the toffee filling:
50 g/2 oz butter
50 g/2 oz soft light
    brown sugar

For the chocolate topping:
397 g can condensed milk
75 g/3 oz plain dark chocolate
75 g/3 oz milk chocolate
75 g/3 oz white chocolate

Preheat the oven to 180°C/350°F/Gas Mark 4, 10 minutes before baking. Oil and line a 20.5 cm /8 inch square cake tin with nonstick baking parchment. Cream the butter and sugar until light and fluffy then sift in the flour and cocoa powder. Add the semolina and mix together to form a soft dough. Press into the base of the prepared tin. Prick all over with a fork, then bake in the preheated oven for 25 minutes. Leave to cool.

To make the toffee filling, gently heat the butter, sugar and condensed milk together until the sugar has dissolved. Bring to the boil, then simmer for 5 minutes, stirring constantly. Leave for 1 minute, then spread over the shortbread and leave to cool.

For the topping, place the different chocolates in separate heatproof bowls and melt one at a time, set over a saucepan of almost boiling water. Drop spoonfuls of each on top of the toffee and tilt the tin to cover evenly. Swirl with a knife for a marbled effect.

Leave the chocolate to cool. When just set mark into fingers using a sharp knife. Leave for at least 1 hour to harden before cutting into fingers.

Try This: FOR AN ALTERNATIVE: 274 FOR A SAVOURY OPTION: 36

Shortbread Thumbs

MAKES 12

125 g/4 oz self-raising flour
125 g/4 oz butter, softened
25 g/1 oz white vegetable fat
50 g/2 oz granulated sugar

25 g/1 oz cornflour, sifted
5 tbsp cocoa powder, sifted
125 g/4 oz icing sugar
6 assorted coloured glacé

cherries, rinsed, dried
and halved

Preheat the oven to 150°C/300°F/Gas Mark 2, 10 minutes before baking. Lightly oil 2 baking sheets. Sift the flour into a large bowl, cut 75 g/3 oz of the butter and the white vegetable fat into small cubes, add to the flour, then, using your fingertips, rub in until the mixture resembles fine breadcrumbs.

Stir in the granulated sugar, sifted cornflour and 4 tablespoons of cocoa powder and bring the mixture together with your hand to form a soft and pliable dough.

Place on a lightly floured surface and shape into 12 small balls. Place onto the baking sheets at least 5 cm/2 inches apart, then press each one with a clean thumb to make a dent.

Bake in the preheated oven for 20–25 minutes or until light golden brown. Remove from the oven and leave for 1–2 minutes to cool. Transfer to a wire rack and leave until cold.

Sift the icing sugar and the remaining cocoa powder into a bowl and add the remaining softened butter. Blend to form a smooth and spreadable icing with 1–2 tablespoons of hot water. Spread a little icing over the top of each biscuit and place half a cherry on each. Leave until set before serving.

Try This: FOR AN ALTERNATIVE: 236   FOR A SAVOURY OPTION: 40

Whipped Shortbread

MAKES 36

225 g/8 oz butter, softened
75 g/3 oz icing sugar
175 g/6 oz flour

hundreds and thousands
sugar strands
chocolate drops

silver balls
50 g/2 oz icing sugar
2–3 tsp lemon juice

Preheat the oven to 180°C/350°F/Gas Mark 4, 10 minutes before baking. Lightly oil a baking sheet.

Cream the butter and icing sugar until fluffy. Gradually add the flour and continue beating for a further 2–3 minutes until it is smooth and light.

Roll into balls and place on a baking sheet. Cover half of the dough mixture with hundreds and thousands, sugar strands, chocolate drops or silver balls. Keep the other half plain.

Bake in the preheated oven for 6–8 minutes, until the bottoms are lightly browned. Remove from the oven and transfer to a wire rack to cool.

Sift the icing sugar into a small bowl. Add the lemon juice and blend until a smooth icing forms.

Using a small spoon swirl the icing over the cooled plain cookies. Decorate with either the extra hundreds and thousands, chocolate drops or silver balls and serve.

Chocolate Brazil & Polenta Squares

MAKES 9 SQUARES

150 g/5 oz shelled Brazil nuts
150 g/5 oz butter, softened
150 g/5 oz soft light
   brown sugar

2 medium eggs, lightly beaten
75 g/3 oz plain flour
25 g/1 oz cocoa powder
¼ tsp ground cinnamon

1 tsp baking powder
pinch of salt
5 tbsp milk
60 g/2½ oz instant polenta

Preheat the oven to 180°C/350°F/Gas Mark 4, 10 minutes before baking. Oil and line a deep 18 cm/7 inch square tin with nonstick baking parchment. Finely chop 50 g/2 oz of the Brazil nuts and reserve. Roughly chop the remainder.

Cream the butter and sugar together until light and fluffy. Gradually add the eggs, beating well between each addition.

Sift the flour, cocoa powder, cinnamon, baking powder and salt into the creamed mixture and gently fold in using a large metal spoon or spatula.

Add the milk, polenta and the 75 g/3 oz of roughly chopped Brazil nuts. Fold into the mixture.

Turn the mixture into the prepared tin, levelling the surface with the back of the spoon. Sprinkle the reserved 50 g/2 oz of finely chopped Brazil nuts over the top. Bake the cake on the centre shelf of the preheated oven for 45–50 minutes, or until well risen and lightly browned and when a clean skewer inserted into the centre of the cake for a few seconds comes out clean.

Leave the cake in the tin for 10 minutes to cool slightly, then turn out onto a wire rack and leave to cool completely. Cut the cake into 9 equal squares and serve. Store in an airtight container.

Try This: FOR AN ALTERNATIVE: 212 FOR A SAVOURY OPTION: 52

Fig & Chocolate Bars

MAKES 12

125 g/4 oz butter
150 g/5 oz plain flour
50 g/2 oz soft light

brown sugar
225 g/8 oz ready-to-eat
dried figs, halved

juice of ½ a large lemon
1 tsp ground cinnamon
125 g/4 oz plain dark chocolate

Preheat the oven to 180°C/350°F/Gas Mark 4, 10 minutes before baking. Lightly oil a 18 cm/ 7 inch square cake tin. Place the butter and the flour in a large bowl and, using your fingertips, rub the butter into the flour until it resembles fine breadcrumbs.

Stir in the sugar, then using your hand, bring the mixture together to form a smooth dough. Knead until smooth then press the dough into the prepared tin. Lightly prick the base with a fork and bake in the preheated oven for 20–30 minutes or until golden. Remove from the oven and leave the shortbread to cool in the tin until completely cold.

Meanwhile, place the dried figs, lemon juice, 125 ml/4 fl oz water and the ground cinnamon in a saucepan and bring to the boil. Cover and simmer for 20 minutes or until soft, stirring occasionally during cooking. Cool slightly, then purée in a food processor until smooth. Cool, then spread over the cooked shortbread.

Melt the chocolate in a heatproof bowl set over a saucepan of simmering water. Alternatively, melt the chocolate in the microwave, according to the manufacturer's instructions. Stir until smooth, then spread over the top of the fig filling. Leave to become firm, then cut into 12 bars and serve.

Try This: FOR AN ALTERNATIVE: 208   FOR A SAVOURY OPTION: 44

Indulgent
Chocolate Squares

MAKES 16

350 g/12 oz plain
   dark chocolate
175 g/6 oz butter, softened
175 g/6 oz soft light
   brown sugar
175 g/6 oz ground almonds

6 large eggs, separated
3 tbsp cocoa powder, sifted
75 g/3 oz fresh
   brown breadcrumbs
125 ml/4 fl oz double cream
50 g/2 oz white

chocolate, chopped
50 g/2 oz milk
   chocolate, chopped
few freshly sliced
   strawberries, to decorate

Preheat the oven to 180°C/350°F/Gas Mark 4, 10 minutes before baking. Oil and line a deep 20.5 cm/8 inch square cake tin with nonstick baking parchment. Melt 225 g/8 oz of the dark chocolate in a heatproof bowl set over a saucepan of almost boiling water. Stir until smooth, then leave until just cool, but not beginning to set.

Beat the butter and sugar until light and fluffy. Stir in the melted chocolate, ground almonds, egg yolks, cocoa powder and breadcrumbs.

Whisk the egg whites until stiff peaks form, then stir a large spoonful into the chocolate mixture. Gently fold in the rest, then pour the mixture into the prepared tin.

Bake on the centre shelf in the preheated oven for 1¼ hours, or until firm, covering the top with tinfoil after 45 minutes, to prevent it over-browning. Leave in the tin for 20 minutes, then turn out onto a wire rack and leave to cool.

Melt the remaining 125 g/4 oz plain chocolate with the cream in a heatproof bowl set over a saucepan of almost boiling water, stirring occasionally. Leave to cool for 20 minutes or until thickened slightly. Spread the topping over the cake. Scatter over the white and milk chocolate and leave to set. Cut into 16 squares and serve decorated with a few freshly sliced strawberries, then serve.

Try This: FOR AN ALTERNATIVE: 286   FOR A SAVOURY OPTION: 78

Apple & Cinnamon Crumble Bars

MAKES 16

450 g/1 lb Bramley cooking
   apples, roughly chopped
50 g/2 oz raisins
50 g/2 oz caster sugar
1 tsp ground cinnamon

zest of 1 lemon
200 g/7 oz plain flour
250 g/9 oz soft light
   brown sugar
½ tsp bicarbonate of soda

150 g/5 oz rolled oats
150 g/5 oz butter, melted
crème fraîche or whipped
   cream, to serve

Preheat the oven to 190°C/375°F/Gas Mark 5, 10 minutes before baking. Place the apples, raisins, sugar, cinnamon and lemon zest into a saucepan over a low heat. Cover and cook for about 15 minutes, stirring occasionally, until the apple is cooked through. Remove the cover, stir well to break up the apple completely with a wooden spoon.

Cook for a further 15–30 minutes over a very low heat until reduced, thickened and slightly darkened. Allow to cool. Lightly oil and line a 20.5 cm/8 inch square cake tin with greaseproof or baking paper.

Mix together the flour, sugar, bicarbonate of soda, rolled oats and butter until combined well and crumbly. Spread half of the flour mixture into the bottom of the prepared tin and press down. Pour over the apple mixture.

Sprinkle over the remaining flour mixture and press down lightly. Bake in the preheated oven for 30–35 minutes, until golden brown.

Remove from the oven and allow to cool before cutting into slices. Serve the bars warm or cold with crème fraîche or whipped cream.

Try This: FOR AN ALTERNATIVE: 328 FOR A SAVOURY OPTION: 64

Crunchy–topped Citrus Chocolate Slices

MAKES 12 SLICES

175 g/6 oz butter
175 g/6 oz soft light
  brown sugar
finely grated rind of 1 orange
3 medium eggs, lightly beaten
1 tbsp ground almonds

175 g/6 oz self-raising flour
¼ tsp baking powder
125 g/4 oz plain dark
  chocolate, coarsely grated
2 tsp milk

For the crunchy topping:
125 g/4 oz granulated sugar
juice of 2 limes
juice of 1 orange

Preheat the oven to 170°C/325°F/Gas Mark 3, 10 minutes before baking. Oil and line a 28 x 18 x 2.5 cm/11 x 7 x 1 inch cake tin with nonstick baking parchment. Place the butter, sugar and orange rind into a large bowl and cream together until light and fluffy. Gradually add the eggs, beating after each addition, then beat in the ground almonds.

Sift the flour and baking powder into the creamed mixture. Add the grated chocolate and milk, then gently fold in using a metal spoon. Spoon the mixture into the prepared tin.

Bake on the centre shelf of the preheated oven for 35–40 minutes, or until well risen and firm to the touch. Leave in the tin for a few minutes to cool slightly. Turn out onto a wire rack and remove the baking parchment.

Meanwhile, make the crunchy topping. Place the sugar with the lime and orange juices into a small jug and stir together. Drizzle the sugar mixture over the hot cake, ensuring the whole surface is covered. Leave until completely cold, then cut into 12 slices and serve.

Try This: FOR AN ALTERNATIVE: 288   FOR A SAVOURY OPTION: 56

Chocolate Florentines

MAKES 20

125 g/4 oz butter or
   margarine
125 g/4 oz soft light
   brown sugar
1 tbsp double cream
50 g/2 oz blanched almonds,
   roughly chopped

50 g/2 oz hazelnuts,
   roughly chopped
75 g/3 oz sultanas
50 g/2 oz glacé cherries,
   roughly chopped
50 g/2 oz plain, dark
   chocolate, roughly

chopped or broken
50 g/2 oz milk chocolate,
   roughly chopped
   or broken
50 g/2 oz white chocolate,
   roughly chopped
   or broken

Preheat the oven to 180°C/350°F/Gas Mark 4, 10 minutes before baking. Lightly oil a baking sheet. Melt the butter or margarine with the sugar and double cream in a small saucepan over a very low heat. Do not boil. Remove from the heat and stir in the almonds, hazelnuts, sultanas and cherries.

Drop teaspoonfuls of the mixture on to the baking sheet. Transfer to the preheated oven and bake for 10 minutes, until golden.

Leave the biscuits to cool on the baking sheet for about 5 minutes, then carefully transfer to a wire rack to cool.

Melt the plain, milk and white chocolates in separate bowls, either in the microwave following the manufacturers' instructions or in a small bowl, placed over a saucepan of gently simmering water. Spread one-third of the biscuits with the plain chocolate, one-third with the milk chocolate and one-third with the white chocolate. Mark out wavy lines on the chocolate when almost set with the tines of a fork. Or dip some of the biscuits in chocolate to half coat and serve.

Try This: FOR AN ALTERNATIVE: 276   FOR A SAVOURY OPTION: 86

Fruit & Spice Chocolate Slice

MAKES 10 SLICES

350 g/12 oz self-raising flour
1 tsp ground mixed spice
175 g/6 oz butter, chilled
125 g/4 oz plain
   dark chocolate,

roughly chopped
125 g/4 oz dried mixed fruit
75 g/3 oz dried apricots,
   chopped
75 g/3 oz chopped

mixed nuts
175 g/6 oz demerara sugar
2 medium eggs,
   lightly beaten
150 ml/¼ pint milk

Preheat the oven to 180°C/350°F/Gas Mark 4, 10 minutes before baking. Oil and line a deep 18 cm/7 inch square tin with nonstick baking parchment. Sift the flour and mixed spice into a large bowl. Cut the butter into small squares and, using your hands, rub in until the mixture resembles fine breadcrumbs.

Add the chocolate, dried mixed fruit, apricots and nuts to the dry ingredients. Reserve 1 tablespoon of the sugar, then add the rest to the bowl and stir. Add the eggs and half of the milk and mix together, then add enough of the remaining milk to give a soft dropping consistency.

Spoon the mixture into the prepared tin, level the surface with the back of a spoon and sprinkle with the reserved demerara sugar. Bake on the centre shelf of the preheated oven for 50 minutes. Cover the top with tinfoil to prevent the cake from browning too much and bake for a further 30–40 minutes, or until it is firm to the touch and a skewer inserted into the centre of the cake comes out clean.

Leave the cake in the tin for 10 minutes to cool slightly, then turn out onto a wire rack and leave to cool completely. Cut into 10 slices and serve. Store in an airtight container.

Try This: FOR AN ALTERNATIVE: 208   FOR A SAVOURY OPTION: 46

Oatmeal Raisin Cookies

MAKES 24

175 g/6 oz plain flour	½ tsp bicarbonate of soda	1 medium egg, lightly beaten
150 g/5 oz rolled oats	125 g/4 oz soft light-	150 ml/¼ pint vegetable or
1 tsp ground ginger	brown sugar	sunflower oil
½ tsp baking powder	50 g/2 oz raisins	4 tbsp milk

Preheat the oven to 200°C/400°F/Gas Mark 6, 15 minutes before baking. Lightly oil a baking sheet.

Mix together the flour, oats, ground ginger, baking pow-der, bicarbonate of soda, sugar and the raisins in a large bowl.

In another bowl, mix the egg, oil and milk together. Make a well in the centre of the dry ingredients and pour in the egg mixture. Mix the mixture together well with either a fork or a wooden spoon to make a soft but not sticky dough.

Place spoonfuls of the dough well apart on the oiled baking sheet and flatten the tops down slightly with the tines of a fork. Transfer the biscuits to the preheated oven and bake for 10–12 minutes until golden.

Remove from the oven, leave to cool for 2–3 minutes, then transfer the biscuits to a wire rack to cool. Serve when cold or otherwise store in an airtight tin.

Try This: FOR AN ALTERNATIVE: 222   FOR A SAVOURY OPTION: 26

Lemon Bars

MAKES 24

175 g/6 oz flour
125 g/4 oz butter
50 g/2 oz granulated sugar
200 g/7 oz caster sugar

2 tbsp flour
½ tsp baking powder
¼ tsp salt
2 medium eggs, lightly beaten

juice and finely grated rind
of 1 lemon
sifted icing sugar, to
decorate

Preheat the oven to 170°C/325°F/Gas Mark 3, 10 minutes before baking. Lightly oil and line a 20.5 cm/8 inch square cake tin with greaseproof or baking paper.

Rub together the flour and butter until the mixture resembles breadcrumbs. Stir in the granulated sugar and mix. Turn the mixture into the prepared tin and press down firmly. Bake in the preheated oven for 20 minutes, until pale golden.

Meanwhile, in a food processor, mix together the caster sugar, flour, baking powder, salt, eggs, lemon juice and rind until smooth. Pour over the prepared base.

Transfer to the preheated oven and bake for a further 20–25 minutes, until nearly set but still a bit wobbly in the cen-tre. Remove from the oven and cool in the tin on a wire rack.

Dust with icing sugar and cut into squares. Serve cold or store in an airtight tin.

Pecan Caramel Millionaire's Shortbread

MAKES 20

125 g/4 oz butter, softened
2 tbsp smooth peanut butter
75 g/3 oz caster sugar
75 g/3 oz cornflour
175 g/6 oz plain flour

For the topping:
200 g/7 oz caster sugar
125 g/4 oz butter
2 tbsp golden syrup
75 g/3 oz liquid glucose
75 ml/3 fl oz water

400 g can sweetened
    condensed milk
175 g/6 oz pecans,
    roughly chopped
75 g/3 oz plain dark chocolate
1 tbsp butter

Preheat the oven to 180°C/350°F/Gas Mark 4, 10 minutes before baking. Lightly oil and line an 18 cm x 28 cm/7 x 11 inch tin with greaseproof or baking paper.

Cream together the butter, peanut butter and sugar until light. Sift in the cornflour and flour together and mix in to make a smooth dough. Press the mixture into the prepared tin and prick all over with a fork. Bake in the oven for 20 minutes, until just golden. Remove from the oven.

Meanwhile, for the topping, combine the sugar, butter, golden syrup, glucose, water and milk in a heavy-based saucepan. Stir constantly over a low heat without boiling until the sugar has dissolved. Increase the heat, boil steadily, stirring constantly, for about 10 minutes until the mixture turns a golden caramel colour.

Remove the saucepan from the heat and add the pecans. Pour over the shortbread base immediately. Allow to cool, then refrigerate for at least 1 hour.

Break the chocolate into small pieces and put into a heatproof bowl with the butter. Place over a saucepan of barely simmering water, ensuring that the bowl does not come into contact with the water. Leave until melted, then stir together well. Remove the shortbread from the refrigerator and pour the chocolate evenly over the top, spreading thinly to cover. Leave to set, cut into squares and serve.

Try This: FOR AN ALTERNATIVE: 290   FOR A SAVOURY OPTION: 44

Marbled Chocolate Traybake

MAKES 18 SQUARES

175 g/6 oz butter
175 g/6 oz caster sugar
1 tsp vanilla essence
3 medium eggs, lightly beaten
200 g/7 oz self-raising flour

½ tsp baking powder
1 tbsp milk
1½ tbsp cocoa powder

For the chocolate icing:
75 g/3 oz plain dark chocolate, broken into pieces
75 g/3 oz white chocolate, broken into pieces

Preheat the oven to 180°C/350°F/Gas Mark 4, 10 minutes before baking. Oil and line a 28 x 18 x 2.5 cm/11 x 7 x 1 inch cake tin with nonstick baking parchment. Cream the butter, sugar and vanilla essence until light and fluffy. Gradually add the eggs, beating well after each addition. Sift in the flour and baking powder and fold in with the milk.

Spoon half the mixture into the prepared tin, spacing the spoonfuls apart and leaving gaps in between.

Blend the cocoa powder to a smooth paste with 2 tablespoons of warm water. Stir this into the remaining cake mixture. Drop small spoonfuls between the vanilla cake mixture to fill in all the gaps. Use a knife to swirl the mixtures together a little.

Bake on the centre shelf of the preheated oven for 35 minutes, or until well risen and firm to the touch. Leave in the tin for 5 minutes to cool, then turn out onto a wire rack and leave to cool. Remove the parchment.

For the icing, place the plain and white chocolate in separate heatproof bowls and melt each over a saucepan of almost boiling water. Spoon into separate nonstick baking parchment piping bags, snip off the tips and drizzle over the top. Leave to set before cutting into squares.

Try This: FOR AN ALTERNATIVE: 232   FOR A SAVOURY OPTION: 96

Light White Chocolate & Walnut Blondies

MAKES 15

75 g/3 oz unsalted butter
200 g/7 oz demerara sugar
2 large eggs, lightly beaten
1 tsp vanilla essence
2 tbsp milk

125 g/4 oz plain flour,
plus 1 tbsp
1 tsp baking powder
pinch of salt
75 g/3 oz walnuts,

roughly chopped
125 g/4 oz white
chocolate drops
1 tbsp icing sugar

Preheat the oven to 190°C/375°F/Gas Mark 5, 10 minutes before baking. Oil and line a 28 x 18 x 2.5 cm/11 x 7 x 1 inch cake tin with nonstick baking parchment. Place the butter and demerara sugar into a heavy-based saucepan and heat gently until the butter has melted and the sugar has started to dissolve. Remove from the heat and leave to cool.

Place the eggs, vanilla essence and milk in a large bowl and beat together. Stir in the butter and sugar mixture, then sift in the 125 g/4oz of flour, the baking powder and salt. Gently stir the mixture twice.

Toss the walnuts and chocolate drops in the remaining 1 tablespoon of flour to coat. Add to the bowl and stir the ingredients together gently.

Spoon the mixture into the tin and bake on the centre shelf of the preheated oven for 35 minutes, or until the top is firm and slightly crusty. Place the tin on a wire rack and leave to cool.

When completely cold, remove the cake from the tin and lightly dust the top with icing sugar. Cut into 15 blondies, using a sharp knife, and serve.

Try This: FOR AN ALTERNATIVE: 188 FOR A SAVOURY OPTION: 66

Everyday Cakes & Buns

Whisked Sponge Cake

CUTS INTO 6 SLICES

125 g/4 oz plain flour,
   plus 1 tsp
175 g/6 oz caster sugar,
   plus 1 tsp

3 medium eggs
1 tsp vanilla essence
4 tbsp raspberry jam
50 g/2 oz fresh

raspberries, crushed
icing sugar, to dredge

Preheat the oven to 200°C/400°F/Gas Mark 6, 15 minutes before baking. Mix 1 teaspoon of the flour and 1 teaspoon of the sugar together. Lightly oil 2 x 18 cm/7 inch sandwich tins and dust lightly with the sugar and flour.

Place the eggs in a large heatproof bowl. Add the sugar, then place over a saucepan of gently simmering water ensuring that the base of the bowl does not touch the hot water. Using an electric whisk beat the sugar and eggs until they become light and fluffy. (The whisk should leave a trail in the mixture when it is lifted out.)

Remove the bowl from the saucepan of water, add the vanilla essence and continue beating for 2–3 minutes. Sift the flour gently into the egg mixture and using a metal spoon or rubber spatula carefully fold in, taking care not to over mix and remove all the air that has been whisked in.

Divide the mixture between the 2 prepared cake tins. Tap lightly on the work surface to remove any air bubbles. Bake in the preheated oven for 20–25 minutes, or until golden. Test that the cake is ready by gently pressing the centre with a clean finger – it should spring back.

Leave to cool in the tins for 5 minutes, then turn out on to a wire rack. Blend the jam and the crushed raspberries together. When the cakes are cold spread over the jam mixture and sandwich together. Dredge the top with icing sugar and serve.

Try This: FOR AN ALTERNATIVE: 142   FOR A SAVOURY OPTION: 58

Lemon & Ginger Buns

MAKES 15

175 g/6 oz butter or margarine
350 g/12 oz plain flour
2 tsp baking powder
½ tsp ground ginger
pinch of salt

finely grated rind of 1 lemon
175 g/6 oz soft light
   brown sugar
125 g/4 oz sultanas
75 g/3 oz chopped mixed peel

25 g/1 oz stem ginger,
   finely chopped
1 medium egg
juice of 1 lemon

Preheat the oven to 220°C/425°F/Gas Mark 7, 15 minutes before baking. Cut the butter or margarine into small pieces and place in a large bowl. Sift the flour, baking powder, ginger and salt together and add to the butter with the lemon rind.

Using the fingertips rub the butter into the flour and spice mixture until it resembles coarse breadcrumbs. Stir in the sugar, sultanas, chopped mixed peel and stem ginger.

Add the egg and lemon juice to the mixture, then using a round bladed knife stir well to mix. (The mixture should be quite stiff and just holding together.)

Place heaped tablespoons of the mixture on to a lightly oiled baking tray, making sure that the dollops of mixture are well apart. Using a fork rough up the edges of the buns and bake in the preheated oven for 12–15 minutes.

Leave the buns to cool for 5 minutes before transferring to a wire rack until cold, then serve. Otherwise store the buns in an airtight tin and eat within 3–5 days.

Try This: FOR AN ALTERNATIVE: 298   FOR A SAVOURY OPTION: 22

Banana Cake

CUTS INTO 8 SLICES

3 medium-sized ripe bananas
1 tsp lemon juice
150 g/5 oz soft brown sugar
75 g/3 oz butter or margarine

250 g/9 oz self-raising flour
1 tsp ground cinnamon
3 medium eggs
50 g/2 oz walnuts, chopped

1 tsp each ground cinnamon
  and caster sugar,
  to decorate
fresh cream, to serve

Preheat the oven to 190°C/375°F/Gas Mark 5, 10 minutes before baking. Lightly oil and line the base of an 18 cm/7 inch deep round cake tin with greaseproof or baking paper.

Mash 2 of the bananas in a small bowl, sprinkle with the lemon juice and a heaped tablespoon of the sugar. Mix together lightly and reserve.

Gently heat the remaining sugar and butter or margarine in a small saucepan until the butter has just melted. Pour into a small bowl, then allow to cool slightly. Sift the flour and cinnamon into a large bowl and make a well in the centre.

Beat the eggs into the cooled sugar mixture, pour into the well of flour, and mix thoroughly. Gently stir in the mashed banana mixture. Pour half of the mixture into the prepared tin. Thinly slice the remaining banana and arrange over the cake mixture.

Sprinkle over the chopped walnuts, then cover with the remaining cake mixture. Bake in the preheated oven for 50–55 minutes, or until well risen and golden brown. Allow to cool in the tin, turn out and sprinkle with the ground cinnamon and caster sugar. Serve hot or cold with a jug of fresh cream for pouring.

 Try This: FOR AN ALTERNATIVE: 302   FOR A SAVOURY OPTION: 94

Toffee Apple Cake

CUTS INTO 8 SLICES

2 small eating apples, peeled
4 tbsp soft dark brown sugar
175 g/6 oz butter or margarine
175 g/6 oz caster sugar

3 medium eggs
175 g/6 oz self-raising flour
150 ml/¼ pint double cream
2 tbsp icing sugar

½ tsp vanilla essence
½ tsp ground cinnamon

Preheat the oven to 180°C/350°F/Gas Mark 4, 10 minutes before baking time. Lightly oil and line the bases of 2 x 20.5 cm/8 inch sandwich tins with greaseproof or baking paper.

Thinly slice the apples and toss in the brown sugar until well coated. Arrange them over the base of the prepared tins and reserve.

Cream together the butter or margarine and caster sugar until light and fluffy.

Beat the eggs together in a small bowl and gradually beat them into the creamed mixture, beating well between each addition.

Sift the flour into the mixture and using a metal spoon or rubber spatula, fold in. Divide the mixture between the 2 cake tins and level the surface.

Bake in the preheated oven for 25–30 minutes, until golden and well risen. Leave in the tins to cool.

Lightly whip the cream with 1 tablespoon of the icing sugar and vanilla essence. Sandwich the cakes together with the cream. Mix the remaining icing sugar and ground cinnamon together, sprinkle over the top of the cake and serve.

 Try This: FOR AN ALTERNATIVE: 328 FOR A SAVOURY OPTION: 44

Gingerbread

CUTS INTO 8 SLICES

175 g/6 oz butter or margarine
225 g/8 oz black treacle
50 g/2 oz dark muscovado
   sugar

350 g/12 oz plain flour
2 tsp ground ginger
150 ml/¼ pint milk, warmed
2 medium eggs

1 tsp bicarbonate of soda
1 piece of stem ginger
  in syrup
1 tbsp stem ginger syrup

Preheat the oven to 150°C/300°C/Gas Mark 2, 10 minutes before baking. Lightly oil and line the base of a 20.5 cm/8 inch deep round cake tin with greaseproof or baking paper.

In a saucepan gently heat the butter or margarine, black treacle and sugar, stirring occasionally until the butter melts. Leave to cool slightly.

Sift the flour and ground ginger into a large bowl. Make a well in the centre, then pour in the treacle mixture. Reserve 1 tablespoon of the milk, then pour the rest into the treacle mixture. Stir together lightly until mixed. Beat the eggs together, then stir into the mixture.

Dissolve the bicarbonate of soda in the remaining 1 tablespoon of warmed milk and add to the mixture. Beat the mixture until well mixed and free of lumps. Pour into the prepared tin and bake in the preheated oven for 1 hour, or until well risen and a skewer inserted into the centre comes out clean.

Cool in the tin, then remove. Slice the stem ginger into thin slivers and sprinkle over the cake. Drizzle with the syrup and serve.

Try This: FOR AN ALTERNATIVE: 230??? FOR A SAVOURY OPTION: 60

Marble Cake

CUTS INTO 8 SLICES

225 g/8 oz butter or margarine
225 g/8 oz caster sugar
4 medium eggs
225 g/8 oz self-raising

flour, sifted
finely grated rind and
   juice of 1 orange
25 g/1 oz cocoa powder, sifted

For the topping:
zest and juice of 1 orange
1 tbsp granulated sugar

Preheat the oven to 190°C/375°F/Gas Mark 5, 10 minutes before baking. Lightly oil and line the base of an 20.5 cm/8 inch deep round cake tin with greaseproof or baking paper.

In a large bowl, cream the butter or margarine and sugar together until light and fluffy. Beat the eggs together. Beat into the creamed mixture a little at a time, beating well between each addition. When all the egg has been added, fold in the flour with a metal spoon or rubber spatula.

Divide the mixture equally between 2 bowls. Beat the grated orange rind into one of the bowls with a little of the orange juice. Mix the cocoa powder with the remaining orange juice until smooth, then add to the other bowl and beat well.

Spoon the mixture into the prepared tin, in alternate spoonfuls. When all the cake mixture is in the tin, take a skewer and swirl it in the 2 mixtures. Tap the base of the tin on the work surface to level the mixture. Bake in the preheated oven for 50 minutes, or until cooked and a skewer inserted into the centre of the cake comes out clean. Remove from the oven and leave in the tin for a few minutes before cooling on a wire rack. Discard the lining paper.

For the topping, place the orange zest and juice with the granulated sugar in a small saucepan and heat gently until the sugar has dissolved. Bring to the boil and simmer gently for 3–4 minutes, until the juice is syrupy. Pour over the cooled cake and serve when cool. Otherwise, store in an airtight tin.

Try This: FOR AN ALTERNATIVE: 258 FOR A SAVOURY OPTION: 90

Chocolate Chelsea Buns

MAKES 12

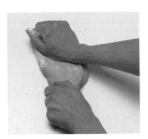

75 g/3 oz dried pears,
finely chopped
1 tbsp apple or orange juice
225 g/8 oz strong plain flour
1 tsp ground cinnamon

½ tsp salt
40 g/1½ oz butter
1½ tsp easy-blend
dried yeast
125 ml/4 fl oz warm milk

1 medium egg,
lightly beaten
75 g/3 oz plain dark
chocolate, chopped
3 tbsp maple syrup

Preheat the oven to 190°C/375°F/Gas Mark 5, 10 minutes before baking. Lightly oil an 18 cm /7 inch square tin. Place the pears in a bowl with the fruit juice, stir then cover and leave to soak while making the dough.

Sift the flour, cinnamon and salt into a bowl, rub in 25 g/1 oz of the butter then stir in the yeast and make a well in the middle. Add the milk and egg and mix to a soft dough. Knead on a floured surface for 10 minutes, until smooth and elastic, then place in a bowl. Cover with clingfilm and leave in a warm place to rise for 1 hour or until doubled in size.

Turn out on a lightly floured surface and knead the dough lightly before rolling out to a rectangle, about 30.5 x 23 cm/12 x 9 inches. Melt the remaining butter and brush over. Spoon the pears and chocolate evenly over the dough leaving a 2.5 cm/1 inch border, then roll up tightly, starting at a long edge. Cut into 12 equal slices, then place, cut-side up in the tin. Cover and leave to rise for 25 minutes, or until doubled in size.

Bake on the centre shelf of the preheated oven for 30 minutes, or until well risen and golden brown. Cover with tinfoil after 20 minutes, if the filling is starting to brown too much.

Brush with the maple syrup while hot, then leave in the tin for 10 minutes to cool slightly. Turn out onto a wire rack and leave to cool. Separate the buns and serve warm.

Try This: FOR AN ALTERNATIVE: 248   FOR A SAVOURY OPTION: 36

Jammy Buns

MAKES 12

175 g/6 oz plain flour	or margarine	1 large egg, beaten
175 g/6 oz wholemeal flour	125 g/4 oz golden	1 tbsp milk
2 tsp baking powder	caster sugar	4–5 tbsp seedless
150 g/5 oz butter	50 g/2 oz dried cranberries	raspberry jam

Preheat the oven to 190°C/375°F/Gas Mark 5, 10 minutes before baking. Lightly oil a large baking sheet.

Sift the flours and baking powder together into a large bowl, then tip in the grains remaining in the sieve. Cut the butter or margarine into small pieces. (It is easier to do this when the butter is in the flour as it helps stop the butter from sticking to the knife.)

Rub the butter into the flours until it resembles coarse breadcrumbs. Stir in the sugar and cranberries. Using a round bladed knife stir in the beaten egg and milk. Mix to form a firm dough. Divide the mixture into 12 and roll into balls.

Place the dough balls on the baking tray, leaving enough space for expansion. Press the thumb into the centre of each ball making a small hollow. Spoon a little of the jam in each hollow. Pinch lightly to seal the tops.

Bake in the preheated oven for 20–25 minutes, or until golden brown. Cool on a wire rack and serve.

Swiss Roll

CUTS INTO 8 SLICES

75 g/3 oz self-raising flour
3 large eggs
1 tsp vanilla essence

90 g/3½ oz caster sugar
25 g/1 oz hazelnuts, toasted
   and finely chopped

3 tbsp apricot conserve
300 ml/½ pint double cream,
   lightly whipped

Preheat the oven to 220°C/425°F/Gas Mark 7, 15 minutes before baking. Lightly oil and line the base of a 23 x 33 cm/9 x 13 inch Swiss roll tin with a single sheet of greaseproof or baking paper.

Sift the flour several times, then reserve on top of the oven to warm a little.

Place a mixing bowl with the eggs, vanilla essence and sugar over a saucepan of hot water, ensuring that the base of the bowl is not touching the water. With the saucepan off the heat whisk with an electric hand whisk until the egg mixture becomes pale and mousse-like and has increased in volume.

Remove the basin from the saucepan and continue to whisk for a further 2–3 minutes. Sift in the flour and very gently fold in using a metal spoon or rubber spatula, trying not to knock out the air whisked in already. Pour into the prepared tin tilting to ensure that the mixture is evenly distributed. Bake in the preheated oven for 10–12 minutes, or until well risen, golden brown and the top springs back when touched lightly with a clean finger.

Sprinkle the toasted, chopped hazelnuts over a large sheet of greaseproof paper. When the cake has cooked turn out on to the hazelnut covered paper and trim the edges of the cake. Holding an edge of the paper with the short side of the cake nearest you, roll the cake up.

When fully cold carefully unroll and spread with the jam and then the cream. Roll back up and serve. Otherwise, store in the refrigerator and eat within 2 days.

Try This: FOR AN ALTERNATIVE: 198   FOR A SAVOURY OPTION: 96

Fudgy & Top Hat Chocolate Buns

MAKES 12

50 g/2 oz self-raising flour
25 g/1 oz cocoa powder
½ tsp baking powder
75 g/3 oz butter, softened
75 g/3 oz soft light
   brown sugar
1 medium egg, lightly beaten
1 tbsp milk

For the fudgy icing:
15 g/½ oz unsalted
   butter, melted
1 tbsp milk
15 g/½ oz cocoa
   powder, sifted
40 g/1½ oz icing sugar, sifted
25 g/1 oz plain dark

For the top hat filling:
150 ml/¼ pint whipping
   cream
2 tsp orange liqueur
1 tbsp icing sugar, sifted
   chocolate, coarsely grated

Preheat the oven to 190°C/375°F/Gas Mark 5, 10 minutes before baking. Sift the flour, cocoa powder and baking powder into a bowl. Add the butter, sugar, egg and milk. Beat for 2–3 minutes or until light and fluffy.

Divide the mixture equally between 12 paper cases arranged in a bun tin tray. Bake on the shelf above the centre in the preheated oven for 15–20 minutes, or until well risen and firm to the touch. Leave in the bun tin for a few minutes, then transfer to a wire rack and leave to cool completely.

For the fudgy icing, mix together the melted butter, milk, cocoa powder and icing sugar. Place a spoonful of icing on the top of 6 of the buns, spreading out to a circle with the back of the spoon. Sprinkle with grated chocolate.

To make the top hats, use a sharp knife to cut and remove a circle of sponge, about 3 cm/1¼ inch across from each of the 6 remaining cakes. Whip the cream, orange liqueur and 1 teaspoon of icing sugar together until soft peaks form.

Spoon the filling into a piping bag fitted with a large star nozzle and pipe a swirl in the centre of each cake. Replace the tops, then dust with the remaining icing sugar and serve with the other buns.

Try This: FOR AN ALTERNATIVE: 228 FOR A SAVOURY OPTION: 48

Chocolate Profiteroles

SERVES 4

For the pastry:
150 ml/¼ pint water
50 g/2 oz butter
65 g/2½ oz plain flour, sifted
2 medium eggs, lightly beaten

For the custard:
300 ml/½ pint milk
pinch of freshly
    grated nutmeg
3 medium egg yolks
50 g/2 oz caster sugar
2 tbsp plain flour, sifted
2 tbsp cornflour, sifted

For the sauce:
175 g/6 oz soft brown sugar
150 ml/¼ pint boiling water
1 tsp instant coffee
1 tbsp cocoa powder
1 tbsp brandy
75 g/3 oz butter
1 tbsp golden syrup

Preheat the oven to 220°C/425°F/Gas Mark 7, 15 minutes before cooking. Lightly oil 2 baking sheets. For the pastry, place the water and the butter in a heavy-based saucepan and bring to the boil. Remove from the heat and beat in the flour. Return to the heat and cook for 1 minute or until the mixture forms a ball in the centre of the saucepan.

Remove from the heat and leave to cool slightly, then gradually beat in the eggs a little at a time, beating well after each addition. Once all the eggs have been added, beat until the paste is smooth and glossy. Pipe or spoon 20 small balls onto the baking sheets, allowing plenty of room for expansion. Bake in the preheated oven for 25 minutes or until well risen and golden brown. Reduce the oven temperature to 180°C/ 350°F/Gas Mark 4. Make a hole in each ball and continue to bake for a further 5 minutes. Remove from the oven and leave to cool.

For the custard, place the milk and nutmeg in a heavy-based saucepan and bring to the boil. In another saucepan, whisk together the egg yolks, sugar and the flours, then beat in the hot milk. Bring to the boil and simmer, whisking constantly for 2 minutes. Cover and leave to cool. Spoon the custard into the profiteroles and arrange on a large serving dish. Place all the sauce ingredients in a small saucepan and bring to the boil, then simmer for 10 minutes. Remove from the heat and cool slightly before serving with the chocolate profiteroles.

Chunky Chocolate Muffins

MAKES 7

50 g/2 oz plain dark chocolate, roughly chopped
50 g/2 oz light muscovado sugar
25 g/1 oz butter, melted
125 ml/4 fl oz milk, heated to room temperature
½ tsp vanilla essence
1 medium egg, lightly beaten
150 g/5 oz self-raising flour
½ tsp baking powder
pinch of salt
75 g/3 oz white chocolate, chopped
2 tsp icing sugar (optional)

Preheat the oven to 200°C/400°F/Gas Mark 6, 15 minutes before baking. Line a muffin or deep bun tin tray with 7 paper muffin cases or oil the individual compartments well. Place the plain chocolate in a large heatproof bowl set over a saucepan of very hot water and stir occasionally until melted. Remove the bowl and leave to cool for a few minutes.

Stir the sugar and butter into the melted chocolate, then the milk, vanilla essence and egg. Sift in the flour, baking powder and salt together. Add the chopped white chocolate, then using a metal spoon, fold together quickly, taking care not to overmix.

Divide the mixture between the paper cases, piling it up in the centre. Bake on the centre shelf of the preheated oven for 20–25 minutes, or until well risen and firm to the touch.

Lightly dust the tops of the muffins with icing sugar as soon as they come out of the oven, if using. Leave the muffins in the tins for a few minutes, then transfer to a wire rack. Serve warm or cold.

Try This: FOR AN ALTERNATIVE: 240   FOR A SAVOURY OPTION: 82

Chocolate & Orange Rock Buns

MAKES 12

200 g/7 oz self-raising flour
25 g/1 oz cocoa powder
½ tsp baking powder
125 g/4 oz butter
40 g/1½ oz granulated sugar
50 g/2 oz candied

pineapple, chopped
50 g/2 oz ready-to-eat dried
    apricots, chopped
50 g/2 oz glacé cherries,
    quartered
1 medium egg

finely grated rind of
    ½ orange
1 tbsp orange juice
2 tbsp demerara sugar

Preheat the oven to 200°C/400°F/Gas Mark 6, 15 minutes before baking. Lightly oil 2 baking sheets, or line them with nonstick baking parchment. Sift the flour, cocoa powder and baking powder into a bowl. Cut the butter into small squares. Add to the dry ingredients, then, using your hands, rub in until the mixture resembles fine breadcrumbs.

Add the granulated sugar, pineapple, apricots and cherries to the bowl and stir to mix. Lightly beat the egg together with the grated orange rind and juice. Drizzle the egg mixture over the dry ingredients and stir to combine. The mixture should be fairly stiff but not too dry, add a little more orange juice, if needed.

Using 2 teaspoons, shape the mixture into 12 rough heaps on the prepared baking sheets. Sprinkle generously with the demerara sugar. Bake in the preheated oven for 15 minutes, switching the baking sheets around after 10 minutes. Leave on the baking sheets for 5 minutes to cool slightly, then transfer to a wire rack to cool. Serve warm or cold.

Try This: FOR AN ALTERNATIVE: 246   FOR A SAVOURY OPTION: 62

Coffee & Pecan Cake

CUTS INTO 8 SLICES

175 g/6 oz self-raising flour
125 g/4 oz butter or margarine
175 g/6 oz golden caster sugar
1 tbsp instant coffee powder
   or granules
2 large eggs

50 g/2 oz pecans,
   roughly chopped

For the icing:
1 tsp instant coffee powder
   or granules

1 tsp cocoa powder
75 g/3 oz unsalted
   butter, softened
175 g/6 oz icing sugar, sifted
whole pecans, to decorate

Preheat the oven to 190°C/375°F/Gas Mark 5, 10 minutes before baking. Lightly oil and line the bases of 2 x 18 cm/7 inch sandwich tins with greaseproof or baking paper. Sift the flour and reserve.

Beat the butter or margarine and sugar together until light and creamy. Dissolve the coffee in 2 tablespoons of hot water and allow to cool. Lightly mix the eggs with the coffee liquid. Gradually beat into the creamed butter and sugar, adding a little of the flour with each addition.

Fold in the pecans, then divide the mixture between the prepared tins and bake in the preheated oven for 20–25 minutes, or until well risen and firm to the touch. Leave to cool in the tins for 5 minutes before turning out and cooling on a wire rack.

To make the icing, blend together the coffee and cocoa powder with enough boiling water to make a stiff paste. Beat into the butter and icing sugar.

Sandwich the 2 cakes together using half of the icing. Spread the remaining icing over the top of the cake and decorate with the whole pecans to serve. Store in an airtight tin.

Try This: FOR AN ALTERNATIVE: 224 FOR A SAVOURY OPTION: 46

Cappuccino Cakes

MAKES 6

125 g/4 oz butter or margarine	1 tbsp strong black coffee	1 tbsp icing sugar, sifted
125 g/4 oz caster sugar	150 g/5 oz self-raising flour	1 tsp vanilla essence
2 medium eggs	125 g/4 oz mascarpone cheese	sifted cocoa powder, to dust

Preheat the oven to 190°C/375°F/Gas Mark 5, 10 minutes before baking. Place 6 large paper muffin cases into a muffin tin or alternatively place on to a baking sheet.

Cream the butter or margarine and sugar together until light and fluffy. Break the eggs into a small bowl and beat lightly with a fork. Using a wooden spoon beat the eggs into the butter and sugar mixture a little at a time, until they are all incorporated.

If the mixture looks curdled beat in a spoonful of the flour to return the mixture to a smooth consistency. Finally beat in the black coffee.

Sift the flour into the mixture, then with a metal spoon or rubber spatula gently fold in the flour. Place spoonfuls of the mixture into the muffin cases. Bake in the preheated oven for 20–25 minutes, or until risen and springy to the touch. Cool on a wire rack.

In a small bowl beat together the mascarpone cheese, icing sugar and vanilla essence. When the cakes are cold, spoon the vanilla mascarpone on to the top of each one. Dust with cocoa powder and serve. Eat within 24 hours and store in the refrigerator.

Try This: FOR AN ALTERNATIVE: 214   FOR A SAVOURY OPTION: 86

Chocolate & Coconut Cake

CUTS INTO 8 SLICES

125 g/4 oz plain
   dark chocolate,
   roughly chopped
175 g/6 oz butter
   or margarine
175 g/6 oz caster sugar

3 medium eggs, beaten
15 g/6 oz self-raising flour
1 tbsp cocoa powder
50 g/2 oz desiccated coconut

For the icing:
125 g/4 oz butter or margarine
2 tbsp creamed coconut
225 g/8 oz icing sugar
25 g/1 oz desiccated
   coconut, lightly toasted

Preheat the oven to 180°C/350°F/Gas Mark 4, 10 minutes before baking. Melt the chocolate in a small bowl placed over a saucepan of gently simmering water, ensuring that the base of the bowl does not touch the water. When the chocolate has melted, stir until smooth and allow to cool.

Lightly oil and line the bases of 2 x 18 cm/7 inch sandwich tins with greaseproof or baking paper. In a large bowl beat the butter or margarine and sugar together with a wooden spoon until light and creamy. Beat in the eggs a little at a time, then stir in the melted chocolate.

Sift the flour and cocoa powder together and gently fold into the chocolate mixture with a metal spoon or rubber spatula. Add the desiccated coconut and mix lightly. Divide between the 2 prepared tins and smooth the tops.

Bake in the preheated oven for 25–30 minutes, or until a skewer comes out clean when inserted into the centre of the cake. Allow to cool in the tin for 5 minutes, then turn out, discard the lining paper and leave on a wire rack until cold.

Beat together the butter or margarine and creamed coconut until light. Add the icing sugar and mix well. Spread half of the icing on 1 cake and press the cakes together. Spread the remaining icing over the top, sprinkle with the coconut and serve.

Try This: FOR AN ALTERNATIVE: 216   FOR A SAVOURY OPTION: 66

Rich Chocolate Cup Cakes

MAKES 12

175 g/6 oz self-raising flour
25 g/1 oz cocoa powder
175 g/6 oz soft light
   brown sugar
75 g/3 oz butter, melted
2 medium eggs, lightly beaten
1 tsp vanilla essence
40 g/1½ oz maraschino

cherries, drained
and chopped

For the chocolate icing:
50 g/2 oz plain dark chocolate
25 g/1 oz unsalted butter
25 g/1 oz icing sugar, sifted

For the cherry icing:
125 g/4 oz icing sugar
7 g/¼ oz unsalted butter,
   melted
1 tsp syrup from the
   maraschino cherries
3 maraschino cherries,
   halved, to decorate

Preheat the oven to 180°C/350°F/Gas Mark 4, 10 minutes before baking. Line a 12 hole muffin or deep bun tin tray with paper muffin cases. Sift the flour and cocoa powder into a bowl. Stir in the sugar, then add the melted butter, eggs and vanilla essence. Beat together with a wooden spoon for 3 minutes or until well blended.

Divide half the mixture between 6 of the paper cases. Dry the cherries thoroughly on absorbent kitchen paper, then fold into the remaining mixture and spoon into the rest of the paper cases.

Bake on the shelf above the centre of the preheated oven for 20 minutes, or until a skewer inserted into the centre of a cake comes out clean. Transfer to a wire rack and leave to cool.

For the chocolate icing, melt the chocolate and butter in a heatproof bowl set over a saucepan of hot water. Remove from the heat and leave to cool for 3 minutes, stirring occasionally. Stir in the icing sugar. Spoon over the 6 plain chocolate cakes and leave to set.

For the cherry icing, sift the icing sugar into a bowl and stir in 1 tablespoon of boiling water, the butter and cherry syrup. Spoon the icing over the remaining 6 cakes, decorate each with a halved cherry and leave to set.

Try This: FOR AN ALTERNATIVE: 242   FOR A SAVOURY OPTION: 82

Lemon Drizzle Cake

CUTS IN 16 SQUARES

| 125 g/4 oz butter or margarine | 2 large eggs | 2 lemons, preferably unwaxed |
| 175 g/6 oz caster sugar | 175 g/6 oz self-raising flour | 50 g/2 oz granulated sugar |

Preheat the oven to 180°C/350°F/Gas Mark 4, 10 minutes before baking. Lightly oil and line the base of an 18 cm/7 inch square cake tin with baking paper. In a large bowl, cream the butter or margarine and sugar together until soft and fluffy.

Beat the eggs, then gradually add a little of the egg to the creamed mixture, adding 1 tablespoon of flour after each addition.

Finely grate the rind from 1 of the lemons and stir into the creamed mixture, beating well until smooth. Squeeze the juice from the lemon, strain, then stir into the mixture. Spoon into the prepared tin, level the surface and bake in the preheated oven for 25–30 minutes. Using a zester remove the peel from the last lemon and mix with 25 g/1 oz of the granulated sugar and reserve.

Squeeze the juice into a small saucepan. Add the rest of the granulated sugar to the lemon juice in the saucepan and heat gently, stirring occasionally. When the sugar has dissolved simmer gently for 3–4 minutes until syrupy.

With a cocktail stick or fine skewer prick the cake all over. Sprinkle the lemon zest and sugar over the top of the cake, drizzle over the syrup and leave to cool in the tin. Cut the cake into squares and serve.

Try This: FOR AN ALTERNATIVE: 254   FOR A SAVOURY OPTION: 50

Victoria Sponge with Mango & Mascarpone

CUTS INTO 8 SLICES

175 g/6 oz caster sugar, plus
    extra for dusting
175 g/6 oz self-raising flour,
    plus extra for dusting

175 g/6 oz butter
    or margarine
3 large eggs
1 tsp vanilla essence

25 g/1 oz icing sugar
250 g/9 oz mascarpone
    cheese
1 large ripe mango, peeled

Preheat the oven to 190°C/375°F/Gas Mark 5, 10 minutes before baking. Lightly oil 2 x 18 cm/7 inch sandwich tins and lightly dust with caster sugar and flour, tapping the tins to remove any excess.

In a large bowl cream the butter or margarine and sugar together with a wooden spoon until light and creamy. In another bowl mix the eggs and vanilla essence together. Sift the flour several times on to a plate. Beat a little egg into the butter and sugar, then a little flour and beat well.

Continue adding the flour and eggs alternately, beating between each addition, until the mixture is well mixed and smooth. Divide the mixture between the 2 prepared cake tins, level the surface, then using the back of a large spoon, make a slight dip in the centre of each cake.

Bake in the preheated oven for 25–30 minutes, until the centre of the cake springs back when gently pressed with a clean finger. Turn out on to a wire rack and leave the cakes until cold.

Beat the icing sugar and mascarpone cheese together, then chop the mango into small cubes. Use half the mascarpone and mango to sandwich the cakes together. Spread the rest of the mascarpone on top, decorate with the remaining mango and serve. Otherwise lightly cover and store in the refrigerator. Use within 3–4 days.

Try This: FOR AN ALTERNATIVE: 336   FOR A SAVOURY OPTION: 34

Fruit Cake

CUTS INTO 10 SLICES

225 g/8 oz butter or margarine
200 g/7 oz soft brown sugar
finely grated rind of 1 orange
1 tbsp black treacle
3 large eggs, beaten
275 g/10 oz plain flour

¼ tsp ground cinnamon
½ tsp mixed spice
pinch of freshly
   grated nutmeg
¼ tsp bicarbonate of soda
75 g/3 oz mixed peel

50 g/2 oz glacé cherries
125 g/4 oz raisins
125 g/4 oz sultanas
125 g/4 oz ready-to-eat dried
   apricots, chopped

Preheat the oven to 150°C/300°C/Gas Mark 2, 10 minutes before baking. Lightly oil and line a 23 cm/9 inch deep round cake tin with a double thickness of greaseproof paper.

In a large bowl cream together the butter or margarine, sugar and orange rind, until light and fluffy, then beat in the treacle. Beat in the eggs a little at a time, beating well between each addition. Reserve 1 tablespoon of the flour. Sift the remaining flour, the spices and bicarbonate of soda into the mixture.

Mix all the fruits and the reserved flour together, then stir into the cake mixture.

Turn into the prepared tin and smooth the top, making a small hollow in the centre of the cake mixture. Bake in the preheated oven for 1 hour, then reduce the heat to 140°C/275°F/ Gas Mark 1.

Bake for a further 1½ hours, or until cooked and a skewer inserted into the centre comes out clean. Leave to cool in the tin, then turn the cake out and serve. Otherwise, when cold store in an airtight tin.

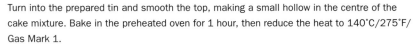

Try This: FOR AN ALTERNATIVE: 250 FOR A SAVOURY OPTION: 76

Chestnut Cake

SERVES 8–10

175 g/6 oz butter, softened
175 g/6 oz caster sugar
250 g can sweetened
   chestnut purée
3 medium eggs, lightly beaten

175 g/6 oz plain flour
1 tsp baking powder
pinch of ground cloves
1 tsp fennel seeds, crushed
75 g/3 oz raisins

50 g/2 oz pine nuts, toasted
125 g/4 oz icing sugar
5 tbsp lemons juice
pared strips of lemon rind,
   to decorate

Preheat oven to 150˚C/300˚F/Gas Mark 2. Oil and line a 23 cm/9 inch springform tin. Beat together the butter and sugar until light and fluffy. Add the chestnut purée and beat. Gradually add the eggs, beating after each addition. Sift in the flour with the baking powder and cloves. Add the fennel seeds and beat. The mixture should drop easily from a wooden spoon when tapped against the side of the bowl. If not, add a little milk.

Beat in the raisins and pine nuts. Spoon the mixture into the prepared tin and smooth the top. Transfer to the centre of the oven and bake in the preheated oven for 55–60 minutes, or until a skewer inserted in the centre of the cake comes out clean. Remove from the oven and leave in the tin.

Meanwhile, mix together the icing sugar and lemon juice in a small saucepan until smooth. Heat gently until hot, but not boiling. Using a cocktail stick or skewer, poke holes into the cake all over. Pour the hot syrup evenly over the cake and leave to soak into the cake. Decorate with pared strips of lemon and serve.

Try This: FOR AN ALTERNATIVE: 176??? FOR A SAVOURY OPTION: 78

Sauternes & Olive Oil Cake

SERVES 8–10

125 g/4 oz plain flour, plus
    extra for dusting
4 medium eggs
125 g/4 oz caster sugar
grated zest of ½ lemon

grated zest of ½ orange
2 tbsp Sauternes or other
    sweet dessert wine
3 tbsp very best quality
    extra-virgin olive oil

4 ripe peaches
1–2 tsp soft brown sugar, or
    to taste
1 tbsp lemon juice
icing sugar, to dust

Preheat the oven to 140°C/275°F/Gas Mark 1. Oil and line a 25.5 cm/10 inch springform tin. Sift the flour on to a large sheet of greaseproof paper and reserve. Using a freestanding electric mixer, if possible, whisk the eggs and sugar together, until pale and stiff. Add the lemon and orange zest.

Turn the speed to low and pour the flour from the paper in a slow, steady stream on to the eggs and sugar mixture. Immediately add the wine and olive oil and switch the machine off as the olive oil should not be incorporated completely.

Using a rubber spatula, fold the mixture very gently 3 or 4 times so that the ingredients are just incorporated. Pour the mixture immediately into the prepared tin and bake in the preheated oven for 20–25 minutes, without opening the door for at least 15 minutes. Test if cooked by pressing the top lightly with a clean finger – if it springs back, remove from the oven, if not, bake for a little longer.

Leave the cake to cool in the tin on a wire rack. Remove the cake from the tin when cool enough to handle.

Meanwhile, skin the peaches and cut into segments. Toss with the brown sugar and lemon juice and reserve. When the cake is cold, dust generously with icing sugar, cut into wedges and serve with the peaches.

Try This: FOR AN ALTERNATIVE: 298 FOR A SAVOURY OPTION: 54

Almond Cake

CUTS INTO 8 SLICES

225 g/8 oz butter
   or margarine
225 g/8 oz caster sugar
3 large eggs

1 tsp vanilla essence
1 tsp almond essence
125 g/4 oz self-raising flour
175 g/6 oz ground almonds

50 g/2 oz whole
   almonds, blanched
25 g/1 oz plain
   dark chocolate

Preheat the oven to 150°C/300°F/Gas Mark 2. Lightly oil and line the base of a 20.5 cm/8 inch deep round cake tin with greaseproof or baking paper.

Cream together the butter or margarine and sugar with a wooden spoon until light and fluffy. Beat the eggs and essences together. Gradually add to the sugar and butter mixture and mix well between each addition.

Sift the flour and mix with the ground almonds. Beat into the egg mixture until mixed well and smooth. Pour into the prepared cake tin.

Roughly chop the whole almonds and scatter over the cake. Bake in the preheated oven for 45 minutes, or until golden and risen and a skewer inserted into the centre of the cake comes out clean.

Remove from the tin and leave to cool on a wire rack. Melt the chocolate in a small bowl placed over a saucepan of gently simmering water, stirring until smooth and free of lumps. Drizzle the melted chocolate over the cooled cake and serve once the chocolate has set.

Try This: FOR AN ALTERNATIVE: 256   FOR A SAVOURY OPTION: 88

Apricot & Almond Layer Cake

CUTS INTO 8–10 SLICES

150 g/5 oz unsalted butter, softened
125 g/4 oz caster sugar
5 medium eggs, separated
150 g/5 oz plain dark chocolate, melted

and cooled
150 g/5 oz self-raising flour, sifted
50 g/2 oz ground almonds
75 g/3 oz icing sugar, sifted
300 g/11 oz apricot jam

1 tbsp amaretto liqueur
125 g/4 oz unsalted butter, melted
125 g/4 oz plain dark chocolate, melted

Preheat the oven to 180°C/350°F/Gas Mark 4, 10 minutes before baking. Lightly oil and line 2 x 23 cm/9 inch round cake tins. Cream the butter and sugar together until light and fluffy, then beat in the egg yolks, one at a time, beating well after each addition. Stir in the cooled chocolate with 1 tablespoon of cooled boiled water, then fold in the flour and ground almonds.

Whisk the egg whites until stiff, then gradually whisk in the icing sugar beating well after each addition. Whisk until the egg whites are stiff and glossy, then fold the egg whites into the chocolate mixture in 2 batches. Divide the mixture evenly between the prepared tins and bake in the preheated oven for 30–40 minutes or until firm. Leave for 5 minutes before turning out onto wire racks. Leave to cool completely.

Split the cakes in half. Gently heat the jam, pass through a sieve and stir in the amaretto liqueur. Place 1 cake layer onto a serving plate. Spread with a little of the jam, then sandwich with the next layer. Repeat with all the layers and use any remaining jam to brush over the entire cake. Leave until the jam sets.

Meanwhile, beat the butter and chocolate together until smooth, then cool at room temperature until thick enough to spread. Cover the top and sides of the cake with the chocolate icing and leave to set before slicing and serving.

Try This: FOR AN ALTERNATIVE: 164   FOR A SAVOURY OPTION: 52

Celebration, Cream Cakes & Gateaux

Buttery Passion Fruit Madeira Cake

CUTS INTO 8–10 SLICES

210 g/7½ oz plain flour
1 tsp baking powder
175 g/6 oz unsalted
    butter, softened
250 g/9 oz caster sugar,

plus 1 tsp
grated zest of 1 orange
1 tsp vanilla essence
3 medium eggs, beaten
2 tbsp milk

6 ripe passion fruits
50 g/2 oz icing sugar
icing sugar, to dust

Preheat the oven to 180°C/350°F/Gas Mark 4, 10 minutes before baking. Lightly oil and line the base of a 23 x 12.5 cm/9 x 5 inch loaf tin with greaseproof paper. Sift the flour and baking powder into a bowl and reserve.

Beat the butter, sugar, orange zest and vanilla essence until light and fluffy, then gradually beat in the eggs, 1 tablespoon at a time, beating well after each addition. If the mixture appears to curdle or separate, beat in a little of the flour mixture. Fold in the flour mixture with the milk until just blended. Do not over mix. Spoon lightly into the prepared tin and smooth the top evenly. Sprinkle lightly with the teaspoon of caster sugar.

Bake in the preheated oven for 55 minutes, or until well risen and golden brown. Remove from the oven and leave to cool for 15–20 minutes. Turn the cake out of the tin and discard the lining paper.

Cut the passion fruits in half and scoop out the pulp into a sieve set over a bowl. Press the juice through using a rubber spatula or wooden spoon. Stir in the icing sugar and stir to dissolve, adding a little extra sugar if necessary.

Using a skewer, pierce holes all over the cake. Slowly spoon the passion fruit glaze over the cake and allow to seep in. Gently invert the cake on to a wire rack, then turn it back the right way up. Dust with icing sugar and cool completely. Serve the Madeira cake cold.

 Try This: FOR AN ALTERNATIVE: 182   FOR A SAVOURY OPTION: 28

Celebration Fruit Cake

CUTS INTO 16 SLICES

125 g/4 oz butter or margarine
125 g/4 oz soft dark
brown sugar
380 g can crushed pineapple
150 g/5 oz raisins
150 g/5 oz sultanas
125 g/4 oz crystallised
ginger, finely chopped

125 g/4 oz glacé cherries,
coarsely chopped
125 g/4 oz mixed cut peel
225 g/8 oz self-raising flour
1 tsp bicarbonate of soda
2 tsp mixed spice
1 tsp ground cinnamon
½ tsp salt
2 large eggs, beaten

For the topping:
100 g/3½ oz pecan or walnut
halves, lightly toasted
125 g/4 oz red, green and
yellow glacé cherries
100 g/3½ oz small pitted
prunes or dates
2 tbsp clear honey

Preheat the oven to 170°C/325°F/Gas Mark 3, 10 minutes before baking. Heat the butter and sugar in a saucepan until the sugar has dissolved, stirring frequently.

Add the pineapple and juice, dried fruits and peel. Bring to the boil, simmer 3 minutes, stirring occasionally, the remove from the heat to cool completely. Lightly oil and line the base of a 20.5 x 7.5 cm/8 x 3 inch loose-bottomed cake tin with non-stick baking paper. Sift the flour, bicarbonate of soda, spices and salt into a bowl.

Add the boiled fruit mixture to the flour with the eggs and mix. Spoon into the tin and smooth the top. Bake in the preheated oven for 1¼ hours, or until a skewer inserted into the centre comes out clean. (If the cake is browning too quickly, cover loosely with tinfoil and reduce the oven temperature.) Remove and cool completely before removing from the tin and discarding the lining paper.

Arrange the nuts, cherries and prunes or dates in an attractive pattern on top of the cake. Heat the honey and brush over the topping to glaze. Alternatively, toss the nuts and fruits in the warm honey and spread evenly over the top of the cake. Cool completely and store in a cake tin for a day or two before serving to allow the flavours to develop.

Try This: FOR AN ALTERNATIVE: 302   FOR A SAVOURY OPTION: 94

Chocolate
Buttermilk Cake

CUTS INTO 8–10 SLICES

175 g/6 oz butter
1 tsp vanilla essence
350 g/12 oz caster sugar
4 medium eggs, separated

100 g/3½ oz self-raising flour
40 g/1½ oz cocoa powder
175 ml/6 fl oz buttermilk
200 g/7 oz plain dark chocolate

100 g/3½ oz butter
300 ml/½ pint double cream

Preheat the oven to 180°C/350°F/Gas Mark 4, 10 minutes before baking. Lightly oil and line a deep 23 cm/9 inch round cake tin. Cream together the butter, vanilla essence and sugar until light and fluffy, then beat in the egg yolks, 1 at a time.

Sift together the flour and cocoa powder and fold into the egg mixture together with the buttermilk. Whisk the egg whites until soft peaks form and fold carefully into the chocolate mixture in 2 batches. Spoon the mixture into the prepared tin and bake in the preheated oven for 1 hour or until firm. Cool slightly, then turn out onto a wire rack and leave until completely cold.

Place the chocolate and butter together in a heatproof bowl set over a saucepan of simmering water and heat until melted. Stir until smooth, then leave at room temperature until the chocolate is thick enough to spread.

Split the cake horizontally in half. Use some of the chocolate mixture to sandwich the 2 halves together. Spread and decorate the top of the cake with the remaining chocolate mixture. Finally, whip the cream until soft peaks form and use to spread around the sides of the cake. Chill in the refrigerator until required. Serve cut into slices. Store in the refrigerator.

Try This: FOR AN ALTERNATIVE: 310   FOR A SAVOURY OPTION: 62

Fresh Strawberry Sponge Cake

8–10 SERVINGS

175 g/6 oz unsalted
  butter, softened
175 g/6 oz caster sugar
1 tsp vanilla essence

3 large eggs, beaten
175 g/6 oz self-raising flour
150 ml/¼ pint double cream
2 tbsp icing sugar, sifted

225 g/8 oz fresh strawberries,
  hulled and chopped
few extra strawberries,
  to decorate

Preheat the oven to 190°C/375°F/Gas Mark 5, 10 minutes before baking. Lightly oil and line the bases of 2 x 20.5 cm/8 inch round cake tins with greaseproof or baking paper.

Using an electric whisk, beat the butter, sugar and vanilla essence until pale and fluffy. Gradually beat in the eggs a little at a time, beating well between each addition. Sift half the flour over the mixture and using a metal spoon or rubber spatula gently fold into the mixture. Sift over the remaining flour and fold in until just blended.

Divide the mixture between the tins evenly. Gently smooth the surfaces with the back of a spoon. Bake in the centre of the preheated oven for 20–25 minutes, or until well risen and golden. Remove and leave to cool before turning out on to a wire rack.

Whip the cream with 1 tablespoon of the icing sugar until it forms soft peaks. Fold in the chopped strawberries. Spread 1 cake layer evenly with the mixture and top with the second cake layer, rounded side up.

Thickly dust the cake with icing sugar and decorate with the reserved strawberries. Carefully slide on to a serving plate and serve.

White Chocolate
& Raspberry Mousse Gateau

CUT 8 SLICES

4 medium eggs
125 g/4 oz caster sugar
75 g/3 oz plain flour, sifted
25 g/1 oz cornflour, sifted
3 gelatine leaves
450 g/1 lb raspberries,

thawed if frozen
400 g/14 oz white chocolate
200 g/7 oz plain fromage frais
2 medium egg whites
25 g/1 oz caster sugar
4 tbsp raspberry or

orange liqueur
200 ml/7 fl oz double cream
fresh raspberries, halved,
to decorate

Preheat the oven to 190°C/375°F/Gas Mark 5, 10 minutes before baking. Oil and line 2 x 23 cm/9 inch cake tins. Whisk the eggs and sugar until thick and creamy and the whisk leaves a trail in the mixture. Fold in the flour and cornflour, then divide between the tins. Bake in the preheated oven for 12–15 minutes or until risen and firm. Cool in the tins, then turn out onto wire racks.

Place the gelatine with 4 tablespoons of cold water in a dish and leave to soften for 5 minutes. Purée half the raspberries, press through a sieve, then heat until nearly boiling. Squeeze out excess water from the gelatine, add to the purée and stir until dissolved. Reserve. Melt 175 g/6 oz of the chocolate in a bowl set over a saucepan of simmering water. Leave to cool, then stir in the fromage frais and purée. Whisk the egg whites until stiff and whisk in the sugar. Fold into the raspberry mixture with the rest of the raspberries.

Line the sides of a 23 cm/9 inch springform tin with nonstick baking parchment. Place 1 layer of sponge in the base and sprinkle with half the liqueur. Pour in the raspberry mixture and top with the second sponge. Brush with the remaining liqueur. Press down and chill in the refrigerator for 4 hours. Unmould onto a plate. Cut a strip of double thickness nonstick baking parchment to fit around the cake and stand 1 cm/½ inch higher. Melt the remaining white chocolate and spread thickly onto the parchment. Leave until just setting. Wrap around the cake and freeze for 15 minutes. Peel away the parchment. Whip the cream until thick and spread over the top. Decorate with raspberries.

Try This: FOR AN ALTERNATIVE: 344 FOR A SAVOURY OPTION: 68

Almond Angel Cake with Amaretto Cream

CUTS INTO 8–10 SLICES

175 g/6 oz icing sugar, plus
   2–3 tbsp
150 g/5 oz plain flour
350 ml/12 fl oz egg whites
   (about 10 large egg whites)

1½ tsp cream of tartar
½ tsp vanilla essence
1 tsp almond essence
¼ tsp salt
200 g/7 oz caster sugar

175 ml/6 fl oz double cream
2 tablespoons Amaretto
   liqueur
fresh raspberries, to decorate

Preheat the oven to 180°C/350°F/Gas Mark 4, 10 minutes before baking. Sift together the 175 g/6 oz icing sugar and flour. Stir to blend, then sift again and reserve.

Using an electric whisk, beat the egg whites, cream of tartar, vanilla essence, ½ teaspoon of almond essence and salt on medium speed until soft peaks form. Gradually add the caster sugar, 2 tablespoons at a time, beating well after each addition, until stiff peaks form. Sift about one-third of the flour mixture over the egg white mixture and using a metal spoon or rubber spatula, gently fold into the egg white mixture. Repeat, folding the flour mixture into the egg white mixture in 2 more batches. Spoon gently into an ungreased angel food cake tin or 25.5 cm/10 inch tube tin.

Bake in the preheated oven until risen and golden on top and the surface springs back quickly when gently pressed with a clean finger. Immediately invert the cake tin and cool completely in the tin. When cool, carefully run a sharp knife around the edge of the tin and the centre ring to loosen the cake from the edge. Using the fingertips, ease the cake from the tin and invert on to a cake plate. Thickly dust the cake with the extra icing sugar.

Whip the cream with the remaining almond essence, Amaretto liqueur and a little more icing sugar, until soft peaks form. Fill a piping bag fitted with a star nozzle with half the cream and pipe around the bottom edge of the cake. Decorate the edge with the fresh raspberries and serve the remaining cream separately.

Chocolate Hazelnut Meringue Gateau

CUTS INTO 8–10 SLICES

5 medium egg whites
275 g/10 oz caster sugar
125 g/4 oz hazelnuts, toasted
and finely chopped

175 g/6 oz plain dark chocolate
100 g/3½ oz butter
3 medium eggs, separated
plus 1 medium egg white

25 g/1 oz icing sugar
125 ml/4 fl oz double cream
hazelnuts, toasted and
chopped, to decorate

Preheat the oven to 150°C/300°F/Gas Mark 2, 5 minutes before baking. Cut 3 pieces of nonstick baking parchment into 30.5 cm x 12.5 cm/12 inch x 5 inch rectangles and then place onto 2 or 3 baking sheets.

Whisk the egg whites until stiff, add half the sugar and whisk until the mixture is stiff, smooth and glossy. Whisk in the remaining sugar, 1 tablespoon at a time, beating well between each addition. When all the sugar has been added whisk for 1 minute. Stir in the hazelnuts. Spoon the meringue inside the marked rectangles spreading in a continuous backwards and forwards movement. Bake in the preheated oven for 1¼ hours, remove and leave until cold. Trim the meringues until they measure 25.5 cm x 10 cm/10 inch x 4 inch.

Melt the chocolate and the butter in a heatproof bowl set over a saucepan of gently simmering water and stir until smooth. Remove from the heat and beat in the egg yolks. Whisk the egg whites until stiff, then whisk in the icing sugar a little at a time. Fold the egg whites into the chocolate mixture and chill in the refrigerator for 20–30 minutes, until thick enough to spread. Whip the double cream until soft peaks form. Reserve.

Place 1 of the meringue layers onto a serving plate. Spread with about half of the mousse mixture, then top with a second meringue layer. Spread the remaining mouse mixture over and top with the third meringue. Spread the cream over the top and sprinkle with the chopped hazelnuts. Chill in the refrigerator for at least 4 hours and up to 24 hours. Serve cut into slices.

Try This: FOR AN ALTERNATIVE: 222   FOR A SAVOURY OPTION: 42

Autumn Bramley Apple Cake

CUTS INTO 8–10 SLICES

225 g/8 oz self-raising flour
1½ tsp baking powder
150 g/5 oz margarine,
    softened
150 g/5 oz caster sugar, plus

extra for sprinkling
1 tsp vanilla essence
2 large eggs, beaten
1.1 kg/2½ lbs Bramley
    cooking apples, peeled,

cored and sliced
1 tbsp lemon juice
½ tsp ground cinnamon
fresh custard sauce or
    cream, to serve

Preheat the oven to 170°C/325°F/Gas Mark 3, 10 minutes before baking. Lightly oil and line the base of a 20.5 cm/8 inch deep cake tin with non-stick baking or greaseproof paper. Sift the flour and baking powder into a small bowl.

Beat the margarine, sugar and vanilla essence until light and fluffy. Gradually beat in the eggs a little at a time, beating well after each addition. Stir in the flour.

Spoon about one-third of the mixture into the tin, smoothing the surface. Toss the apple slices in the lemon juice and cinnamon and spoon over the cake mixture, making a thick even layer. Spread the remaining mixture over the apple layer to the edge of the tin, making sure the apples are covered. Smooth the top with the back of a wet spoon and sprinkle generously with sugar.

Bake in the preheated oven for 1½ hours, or until well risen and golden, the apples are tender and the centre of the cake springs back when pressed lightly. (Reduce the oven temperature slightly and cover the cake loosely with tinfoil if the top browns too quickly.)

Transfer to a wire rack and cool for about 20 minutes in the tin. Run a thin knife blade between the cake and the the tin to loosen the cake and invert on to a paper-lined rack. Turn the cake the right way up and cool. Serve with the custard sauce or cream.

Try This: FOR AN ALTERNATIVE: 270   FOR A SAVOURY OPTION: 98

Chocolate Roulade

CUTS INTO 8 SLICES

200 g/7 oz plain dark chocolate
200 g/7 oz caster sugar
7 medium eggs, separated
300 ml/½ pint double cream

3 tbsp Cointreau or
   Grand Marnier
4 tbsp icing sugar for dusting

To decorate:
fresh raspberries
sprigs of fresh mint

Preheat the oven to 180°C/350°F/Gas Mark 4, 10 minutes before baking. Lightly oil and line a 33 cm x 23 cm/13 inch x 9 inch Swiss roll tin with nonstick baking parchment. Break the chocolate into small pieces into a heatproof bowl set over a saucepan of simmering water. Leave until almost melted, stirring occasionally. Remove from the heat and leave to stand for 5 minutes.

Whisk the egg yolks with the sugar until pale and creamy and the whisk leaves a trail in the mixture when lifted, then carefully fold in the melted chocolate.

In a clean grease-free bowl, whisk the egg whites until stiff, then fold 1 large spoonful into the chocolate mixture. Mix lightly, then gently fold in the remaining egg whites. Pour the mixture into the prepared tin and level the surface. Bake in the oven for 20–25 minutes or until firm.

Remove the cake from the oven, leave in the tin and cover with a wire rack and a damp tea towel. Leave for 8 hours or preferably overnight.

Dust a large sheet of nonstick baking parchment generously with 2 tablespoons of the icing sugar. Unwrap the cake and turn out onto the greaseproof paper. Remove the baking parchment. Whip the cream with the liqueur until soft peaks form. Spread over the cake, leaving a 2.5 cm /1 inch border all round.

Using the paper to help, roll the cake up from a short end. Transfer to a serving plate, seam-side down, and dust with the remaining icing sugar. Decorate with fresh raspberries and mint. Serve.

Try This: FOR AN ALTERNATIVE: 276 FOR A SAVOURY OPTION: 56

Lemony Coconut Cake

CUTS INTO 10-12 SLICES

275 g/10 oz plain flour
2 tbsp cornflour
1 tbsp baking powder
1 tsp salt
150 g/5 oz white vegetable
    fat or soft margarine
275 g/10 oz caster sugar
grated zest of 2 lemons

1 tsp vanilla essence
3 large eggs
150 ml/¼ pint milk
4 tbsp Malibu or rum
450 g/1 lb jar lemon curd
lime zest, to decorate

For the frosting:
275 g/10 oz caster sugar
125 ml/4 fl oz water
1 tbsp glucose
¼ tsp salt
1 tsp vanilla essence
3 large egg whites
75 g/3 oz shredded coconut

Preheat the oven to 180°C/350°F/Gas Mark 4, 10 minutes before baking. Lightly oil and flour 2 x 20.5 cm/8 inch non-stick cake tins. Sift the flour, cornflour, baking powder and salt into a large bowl and add the white vegetable fat or margarine, sugar, lemon zest, vanilla essence, eggs and milk. With an electric whisk on a low speed, beat until blended, adding a little extra milk if the mixture is very stiff. Increase the speed to medium and beat for about 2 minutes. Divide the mixture between the tins and smooth the tops evenly. Bake in the oven for 20–25 minutes, or until the cakes feel firm and are cooked. Remove from the oven and cool before removing from the tins.

Put all the ingredients for the frosting, except the coconut, into a heatproof bowl placed over a saucepan of simmering water. (Do not allow the base of the bowl to touch the water.) Using an electric whisk, blend the frosting ingredients on a low speed. Increase the speed to high and beat for 7 minutes, until the whites are stiff and glossy. Remove the bowl from the heat and continue beating until cool. Cover with clingfilm.

Using a serrated knife, split the cake layers horizontally in half and sprinkle each cut surface with the Malibu or rum. Sandwich the cakes together with the lemon curd and press lightly. Spread the top and sides with the frosting, swirling and peaking the top. Sprinkle the coconut over the top of the cake and gently press on to the sides to cover. Decorate the cake with the lime zest and serve.

Italian Polenta Cake
with Mascarpone Cream

CUTS INTO 6–8 SLICES

1 tsp butter and flour for
   the tin
100 g/3½ oz plain flour
40 g/1½ oz polenta or
   yellow cornmeal
1 tsp baking powder
¼ tsp salt
grated zest of 1 lemon
2 large eggs

150 g/5 oz caster sugar
5 tbsp milk
½ tsp almond essence
2 tbsp raisins or sultanas
75 g/3 oz unsalted
   butter, softened
2 medium dessert pears,
   peeled, cored and
   thinly sliced

2 tbsp apricot jam
175 g/6 oz mascarpone cheese
1–2 tsp sugar
50 ml/2 fl oz double cream
2 tbsp Amaretto liqueur
   or rum
2–3 tbsp toasted flaked
   almonds
icing sugar, to dust

Preheat the oven to 190°C/375°F/Gas Mark 5, 10 minutes before baking. Butter a 23 cm/
9 inch springform tin. Dust lightly with flour.

Stir the flour, polenta or cornmeal, baking powder, salt and lemon zest together. Beat the eggs
and half the sugar until light and fluffy. Slowly beat in the milk and almond essence. Stir in the
raisins or sultanas, then beat in the flour mixture and 50 g/2 oz of the butter. Spoon into the
tin and smooth the top evenly. Arrange the pear slices on top in overlapping concentric circles.

Melt the remaining butter and brush over the pear slices. Sprinkle with the rest of the sugar.
Bake in the preheated oven for about 40 minutes, until puffed and golden and the edges of the
pears are lightly caramelised. Transfer to a wire rack. Reserve to cool in the tin for 15 minutes.

Remove the cake from the tin. Heat the apricot jam with 1 tablespoon of water and brush over
the top of the cake to glaze. Beat the mascarpone cheese with the sugar to taste, the cream and
Amaretto or rum until smooth and forming a soft dropping consistency. When cool, sprinkle the
almonds over the polenta cake and dust with the icing sugar. Serve the cake with the liqueur-
flavoured mascarpone cream.

Try This: FOR AN ALTERNATIVE: 292 FOR A SAVOURY OPTION: 46

Chocolate Mousse Sponge

CUTS INTO 8–10 SLICES

3 medium eggs
75 g/3 oz caster sugar
1 tsp vanilla essence
50 g/2 oz self-raising
 flour, sifted
25 g/1 oz ground almonds
50 g/2 oz plain dark

chocolate, grated
icing sugar, for dusting
freshly sliced strawberries,
 to decorate

For the mousse:
2 sheets gelatine

50 ml/2 fl oz double cream
100 g/3½ oz plain dark
 chocolate, chopped
1 tsp vanilla essence
4 medium egg whites
125 g/4 oz caster sugar

Preheat the oven to 180°C/350°F/Gas Mark 4, 10 minutes before baking. Lightly oil and line a 23 cm/9 inch round cake tin and lightly oil the sides of a 23 cm/9 inch springform tin. Whisk the eggs, sugar and vanilla essence until thick and creamy. Fold in the flour, ground almonds and dark chocolate. Spoon the mixture into the prepared round cake tin and bake in the preheated oven for 25 minutes or until firm. Turn out onto a wire rack to cool.

For the mousse, soak the gelatine in 50 ml/2 fl oz of cold water for 5 minutes until softened. Meanwhile, heat the double cream in a small saucepan, when almost boiling, remove from the heat and stir in the chocolate and vanilla essence. Stir until the chocolate melts. Squeeze the excess water out of the gelatine and add to the chocolate mixture. Stir until dissolved, then pour into a large bowl. Whisk the egg whites until stiff, then gradually add the caster sugar, whisking well between each addition. Fold the egg white mixture into the chocolate mixture in 2 batches.

Split the cake into 2 layers. Place 1 layer in the bottom of the springform tin. Pour in the chocolate mousse mixture, then top with the second layer of cake. Chill in the refrigerator for 4 hours or until the mousse has set. Loosen the sides and remove the cake from the tin. Dust with icing sugar and decorate the top with a few freshly sliced strawberries. Serve cut into slices.

Try This: FOR AN ALTERNATIVE: 230 FOR A SAVOURY OPTION: 76

Mocha Truffle Cake

CUTS INTO 8–10 SLICES

3 medium eggs
125 g/4 oz caster sugar
40 g/1½ oz cornflour
40 g/1½ oz self-raising flour
2 tbsp cocoa powder

2 tbsp milk
2 tbsp coffee liqueur
100 g/3½ oz white chocolate,
 melted and cooled
200 g/7 oz plain dark

chocolate, melted
 and cooled
600 ml/1 pint double cream
200 g/7 oz milk chocolate
100 g/3½ oz unsalted butter

Preheat the oven to 180°C/350°F/Gas Mark 4, 10 minutes before cooking. Lightly oil and line a deep 23 cm/9 inch round cake tin. Beat the eggs and sugar in a bowl until thick and creamy.

Sift together the cornflour, self-raising flour and cocoa powder and fold lightly into the egg mixture. Spoon into the prepared tin and bake in the preheated oven for 30 minutes or until firm.

Turn out onto a wire rack and leave until cold. Split the cold cake horizontally into 2 layers. Mix together the milk and coffee liqueur and brush onto the cake layers.

Stir the cooled white chocolate into one bowl and the cooled plain dark chocolate into another one. Whip the cream until soft peaks form, then divide between the 2 bowls and stir. Place 1 layer of cake in a 23 cm/9 inch springform tin. Spread with half the white chocolate cream. Top with the dark chocolate cream, then the remaining white chocolate cream, finally place the remaining cake layer on top. Chill in the refrigerator for 4 hours or overnight until set.

When ready to serve, melt the milk chocolate and butter in a heatproof bowl set over a saucepan of simmering water and stir until smooth. Remove from the heat and leave until thick enough to spread, then use to cover the top and sides of the cake. Leave to set at room temperature, then chill in the refrigerator. Cut the cake into slices and serve.

Try This: FOR AN ALTERNATIVE: 198   FOR A SAVOURY OPTION: 34

Rich Devil's Food Cake

CUTS INTO 12–16 SLICES

450 g/1 lb plain flour
1 tbsp bicarbonate of soda
½ tsp salt
75 g/3 oz cocoa powder
300 ml/½ pint milk
150 g/5 oz butter, softened
400 g/14 oz soft dark

brown sugar
2 tsp vanilla essence
4 large eggs

Chocolate fudge frosting:
275 g/10 oz caster sugar
½ tsp salt

125 g/4 oz plain dark
chocolate, chopped
225 ml/8 fl oz milk
2 tbsp golden syrup
125 g/4 oz butter, diced
2 tsp vanilla essence

Preheat the oven to 180°C/350°F/Gas Mark 4, 10 minutes before baking. Lightly oil and line the bases of 3 x 23 cm/9 inch cake tins with greaseproof or baking paper. Sift the flour, bicarbonate of soda and salt into a bowl.

Sift the cocoa powder into another bowl and gradually whisk in a little of the milk to form a paste. Continue whisking in the milk until a smooth mixture results. Beat the butter, sugar and vanilla essence until light and fluffy then gradually beat in the eggs, beating well after each addition. Stir in the flour and cocoa mixtures alternately in 3 or 4 batches. Divide the mixture evenly among the tins, smoothing the surfaces. Bake in the preheated oven for 25–35 minutes, until cooked and firm to the touch. Remove, cool and turn out on to a wire rack. Discard the lining paper.

To make the frosting, put the sugar, salt and chocolate into a heavy-based saucepan and stir in the milk until blended. Add the golden syrup and butter. Bring the mixture to the boil over a medium-high heat, stirring to help dissolve the sugar. Boil for 1 minute, stirring constantly. Remove from the heat, stir in the vanilla essence and cool. When cool, whisk until thickened and slightly lightened in colour.

Sandwich the 3 cake layers together using a third of the frosting, placing the third cake layer with the flat side up. Transfer the cake to a serving plate and, using a metal palette knife, spread the remaining frosting over the top and sides. Swirl the top to give a decorative effect and serve.

Try This: FOR AN ALTERNATIVE: 318   FOR A SAVOURY OPTION: 70???

Luxury Carrot Cake

CUTS INTO 12 SLICES

275 g/10 oz plain flour
2 tsp baking powder
1 tsp bicarbonate of soda
1 tsp salt
2 tsp ground cinnamon
1 tsp ground ginger
200 g/7 oz dark soft
 brown sugar
100 g/3½ oz caster sugar

4 large eggs, beaten
250 ml/9 fl oz sunflower oil
1 tbsp vanilla essence
4 carrots, peeled and
 shredded (about 450 g/1 lb)
380 g/14 oz can crushed
 pineapple, well drained
125 g/4 oz pecans or walnuts,
 toasted and chopped

For the frosting:
175 g/6 oz cream cheese,
 softened
50 g/2 oz butter, softened
1 tsp vanilla essence
225 g/8 oz icing sugar, sifted
1–2 tbsp milk

Preheat the oven to 180°C/350°F/Gas Mark 4, 10 minutes before baking. Lightly oil a 33 x 23 cm /13 x 9 inch baking tin. Line the base with non-stick baking paper, oil and dust with flour.

Sift the first 6 ingredients into a large bowl and stir in the sugars to blend. Make a well in the centre. Beat the eggs, oil and vanilla essence together and pour into the well. Using an electric whisk, gradually beat drawing in the flour mixture from the side until a smooth batter forms.

Stir in the carrots, crushed pineapple and chopped nuts until blended. Pour into the prepared tin and smooth the surface evenly. Bake in the preheated oven for 50 minutes, or until firm and a skewer inserted into the centre comes out clean. Remove from the oven and leave to cool before removing from the tin and discarding the lining paper.

For the frosting, beat the cream cheese, butter and vanilla essence together until smooth, then gradually beat in the icing sugar until the frosting is smooth. Add a little milk, if necessary. Spread the frosting over the top. Refrigerate for about 1 hour to set the frosting, then cut into squares and serve.

Try This: FOR AN ALTERNATIVE: 268   FOR A SAVOURY OPTION: 96

Black Forest Gateau

CUTS 10–12 SLICES

250 g/9 oz butter
1 tbsp instant coffee
   granules
350 ml/12 fl oz hot water
200 g/7 oz plain dark
   chocolate, chopped

or broken
400 g/14 oz caster sugar
225 g/8 oz self-raising flour
150 g/5 oz plain flour
50 g/2 oz cocoa powder
2 medium eggs

2 tsp vanilla essence
2 x 400 g cans stoned
   cherries in juice
2 tsp arrowroot
600 ml/1 pint double cream
50 ml/2 fl oz kirsch

Preheat the oven to 150˚C/300˚F/Gas Mark 2, 5 minutes before serving. Lightly oil and line a deep 23 cm/9 inch cake tin. Melt the butter in a large saucepan. Blend the coffee with the hot water, add to the butter with the chocolate and sugar and heat gently, stirring until smooth. Pour into a large bowl and leave until just warm.

Sift together the flours and cocoa powder. Using an electric mixer, whisk the warm chocolate mixture on a low speed, then gradually whisk in the dry ingredients. Whisk in the eggs 1 at a time, then the vanilla essence. Pour the mixture into the prepared tin and bake in the preheated oven for 1 hour 45 minutes or until firm and a skewer inserted into the centre comes out clean. Leave in the tin for 5 minutes to cool slightly before turning out onto a wire rack.

Place the cherries and their juice in a small saucepan and heat gently. Blend the arrowroot with 2 teaspoons of water until smooth, then stir into the cherries. Cook, stirring, until the liquid thickens. Simmer very gently for 2 minutes, then leave until cold.

Whisk the double cream until thick. Trim the top of the cake if necessary, then split the cake into 3 layers. Brush the base of the cake with half the kirsch. Top with a layer of cream and one-third of the cherries. Repeat the layering, then place the third layer on top. Reserve a little cream for decorating and use the remainder to cover the top and sides of the cake. Pipe a decorative edge around the cake, then arrange the remaining cherries in the centre and serve.

Try This: FOR AN ALTERNATIVE: 194   FOR A SAVOURY OPTION: 68

French Chocolate Pecan Torte

CUTS INTO 16 SLICES

200 g/7 oz plain dark
  chocolate, chopped
150 g/5 oz butter, diced
4 large eggs
100 g/3½ oz caster sugar
2 tsp vanilla essence

125 g/4 oz pecans,
  finely ground
2 tsp ground cinnamon
24 pecan halves, lightly
  toasted, to decorate

Chocolate glaze:
125 g/4 oz plain dark
  chocolate, chopped
60 g/2½ oz butter, diced
2 tbsp clear honey
¼ tsp ground cinnamon

Preheat the oven to 180°C/350°F/Gas Mark 4, 10 minutes before baking. Lightly butter and line a 20.5 x 5 cm/8 x 2 inch springform tin with non-stick baking paper. Wrap the tin in a large sheet of tinfoil to prevent water seeping in. Melt the chocolate and butter in a saucepan over a low heat and stir until smooth. Remove from the heat and cool.

Using an electric whisk, beat the eggs, sugar and vanilla essence until light and foamy. Gradually beat in the melted chocolate, ground nuts and cinnamon, then pour into the prepared tin.

Set the foil-wrapped tin in a large roasting tin and pour in enough boiling water to come 2 cm /¾ inches up the sides of the tin. Bake in the preheated oven until the edge is set, but the centre is still soft when the tin is gently shaken. Remove from the oven and place on a wire rack to cool.

For the glaze, melt all the ingredients over a low heat until melted and smooth, then remove from the heat. Dip each pecan halfway into the glaze and set on a sheet of non-stick baking paper until set. Allow the remaining glaze to thicken slightly. Remove the cake from the tin and invert. Pour the glaze over the cake smoothing the top and spreading the glaze around the sides. Arrange the glazed pecans around the edge of the torte. Allow to set and serve.

Raspberry & Hazelnut Meringue Cake

CUTS INTO 8 SLICES

For the meringue:
4 large egg whites
¼ tsp cream of tartar
225 g/8 oz caster sugar
75 g/3 oz hazelnuts, skinned,
toasted and finely ground

For the filling:
300 ml/½ pint double cream
1 tbsp icing sugar

1–2 tbsp raspberry-flavoured
liqueur (optional)
350 g/12 oz fresh raspberries

Preheat the oven to 140°C/275°F/Gas Mark 1. Line 2 baking sheets with non-stick baking paper and draw a 20.5 cm/8 inch circle on each. Whisk the egg whites and cream of tartar until soft peaks form then gradually beat in the sugar, 2 tablespoons at a time. Beat well after each addition until the whites are stiff and glossy. Using a metal spoon or rubber spatula, gently fold in the ground hazelnuts.

Divide the mixture evenly between the 2 circles and spread neatly. Swirl 1 of the circles to make a decorative top layer. Bake in the preheated oven for about 1½ hours, until crisp and dry. Turn off the oven and allow the meringues to cool for 1 hour. Transfer to a wire rack to cool completely. Carefully peel off the papers.

For the filling, whip the cream, icing sugar and liqueur, if using, together until soft peaks form. Place the flat round on a serving plate. Spread over most of the cream, reserving some for decorating and arrange the raspberries in concentric circles over the cream.

Place the swirly meringue on top of the cream and raspberries, pressing down gently. Pipe the remaining cream on to the meringue and decorate with a few raspberries and serve.

Try This: FOR AN ALTERNATIVE: 162   FOR A SAVOURY OPTION: 90

Index

Index